FROM TRASH TO Treasure

Lee Habbershaw

Published by

Fresh Wine Publishing
Adelaide South Australia

© 2020 Lee Habbershaw

All rights reserved. This publication is copyright. Other than for the purposes of and subject to the conditions of the Copyright Act, no part of it may in any form or by any means (electronic, mechanical, microcopying, photocopying, recording or otherwise) be reproduced, stored in a retrieval system or transmitted without prior written permission from the publisher.

Layout & design – Purple Lemon Creative

First printed March 2020

ISBN 978-0-6487959-0-2

A catalogue record for this work is available from the National Library of Australia

DEDICATION

I dedicate "From Trash To Treasure"
to my loving Heavenly Father,
My precious Saviour and Healer, the Lord Jesus Christ
and my wonderful Helper and Friend – Holy Spirit.

Also to my incredible late husband, Alan,
my daughter, Cheryl, her husband Barry
and their five children – Danielle, Paris, Chelsea,
James and Charlie
and my stepson, Jason, his wife Alex
and their five children – Matthew, Monique,
Amber, Jamie and Michael

To all broken and hurting people,
please remember God is no respecter of persons.
What He has done for me He can do for you.
He is such a loving God and willing to bring healing
and restoration to hurting, broken people.

ACKNOWLEDGEMENTS

I would like to acknowledge the Pastors who have sown into our lives and the ministry over many years.

Pastor Andrew Evans - thank you for believing in us as God launched our ministry while we were under the authority of your Church at Paradise. Also for your grace as we launched into the uncharted waters of healing and restoring the soul.

Thanks also to Pastor Dave Peterson formally of Paradise Church who endorsed what God was leading us into, and for acknowledging the outstanding changes in the lives of those who received ministry.

Pastors Beverly and Kevin Dales of Lifeforce Church we thank you so much for believing in us and encouraging us to continue to pursue our calling in God even in the most difficult of times.

Thank you so much to my great Pastors, David and Donna Hall of Revival City Church who have embraced and encouraged me in the work of the ministry.

I am honoured to have received your love, encouragement and support.

CONTENTS

Endorsements	6
Introduction	7
1. Encountering Evil	9
2. Experiencing Heaven	19
3. Finding Real Love	29
4. Life In The Country	37
5. Free At Last	47
6. Birth Of The Ministry	55
7. A Blast From The Past	81
8. Birth Of Christian Counselling College	93
9. Transformed by Power of Holy Spirit	97
10. The Enemy Strikes Again	105
11. The Door To Indonesia Opens	113
12. Alan's Promotion to Glory	125
13. Final Trip To Indonesia	131
14. God Opens New Doors For Ministry	137
15. Conclusion	147
16. Testimonies	151

ENDORSEMENTS

From Trash to Treasure is an intensely honest account of a life powerfully redeemed and is a demonstration of the goodness of God.

Lee Habbershaw's journey to recovery from sexual abuse moved me to tears – sometimes in compassion, but often in joy. The book is rich with the landmark of life events and Biblical truths which, layer by layer, led Lee into the powerful teaching and counselling ministry she operates in today.

This book could change your life.

Rhonda Pooley
M.A., Dip. Ed. Author, teacher & editorial services.

What a privilege it has been to host Lee Habbershaw as she taught on Prayer Ministry. Lee is totally reliant on the Holy Spirit to lead and guide every ministry session, where participants are equipped to minister and support hurting people.

We highly recommend Lee's teaching and training as she ministers to the local Church. This ministry is all about people being made whole - Jesus came to set the captives free in every way: body, soul and spirit.

This is Lee's whole purpose in her ministry. We praise God that her ministry is highly successful.

Ps Trevor and Valmai Auricht
Impact Church, Barossa

The road to healing from trauma and brokenness – and how God leads us through it – is unique for everyone. Lee has given us her story with courage, vulnerability and honesty. Of particular help to the reader, is the practical offer of hope as Lee describes the method of healing, through which God has used her powerfully to minister to broken people.

Deb McKee
Grad Dip Couns & PsychTh
CCAA (Grad) PACFA Reg. Provisional
Purple Lemon Counselling

INTRODUCTION

One day just over forty years ago the Lord Jesus Christ was wandering around in a huge rubbish dump filled with so much stuff that had been thrown away as absolutely worthless. This trash consisted of things that had no value, had no more purpose, useless and simply not wanted by anyone. Jesus was looking intently at this unwanted junk almost as though He was searching for something in particular.

Suddenly He stopped and looked intently at a little old rag doll with dirt all over its face as well as its body. The limbs were lifeless – they were just hanging from the doll's torso. He gently bent down and picked her up and began brushing the dirt from her face. Then Jesus lovingly held this little rag doll against His chest with His loving hands. As He gently continued to hold her in His arms of love an amazing thing happened. This lifeless, unwanted doll began to come to life little by little until there was life in the limbs, a smile on its face and it looked almost like a happy, loved human being.

This is a picture of my life – a worthless, useless, unwanted person with no value, and no purpose. One who had been so hurt and was broken beyond comprehension and disregarded as trash. But one day Jesus came, healed my hurt and brokenness, cleansed me with His Blood, breathed His Life into me and poured out His love on me, claiming me as His treasure. What He did for me, He can do for you too!

Chapter 1
ENCOUNTERING EVIL

How rude, I thought, as I walked away from yet another slammed door. Why can't people just say a polite 'no' when asked if they would like to donate to the 'Down Every Street Appeal' instead of reacting as if I was an axe murderer? Surely they could see I'm harmless - just a high-school student trying to help others less fortunate than myself.

Having completed my allotted territory for collection I began the walk home. I had reached the corner of the street where I lived for the last stretch home when a van pulled up alongside me and the driver asked me if I would like a lift home. 'No thank you' I replied, 'my parents tell me not to take lifts from strangers'. 'But I'm not a stranger,' said the man. 'You know me; my wife goes to the same Church as you do'.

After convincing me he was safe to go with I hopped in the van, but instead of turning the corner into my street he kept going. 'Hey, you missed my corner,' I said. 'I thought we'd just enjoy a little ride', he replied. I began to feel uneasy. 'But I want to go straight home.' I said. 'We won't be long', he responded, and accelerated. The further we travelled away from my home the more uneasy I became. I had to get out of there, but how? The car was moving too fast. Uneasiness became panic as the car pulled up in bush land. I prepared to run, but strong, rough hands dragged me from the passenger's seat to the back of the van.

I began to scream. 'No point doing that' was the gruff response. 'There's nobody around to hear you'. I struggled desperately to get free. His strength was amazing as he tore off my briefs, and unzipped his jeans. What on earth was he doing?

There was a lot of fumbling as I tried to break free and then there was this incredible pain as something entered my body and pushed hard against me. I cried and screamed as the pain and pushing went on forever. Apart from the pain and fear other feelings were aroused which I could not explain. Eventually there was a loud groan and the man's body stopped pounding against mine and lay still. I was sobbing uncontrollably and too scared to move. I was thrust aside and commanded to stop bawling and get back in the front of the car. Without a word he shoved me into the front seat and took off.

As we reached the corner of my street he said, 'Get yourself together and I'll drop you off where I picked you up. And don't mention this to anybody because I will deny it and my word will be believed against yours'. There was a pause and he added, 'And you'll put that mother of yours at risk, too'. Then he pushed me out of the van, throwing my collection tin out after me, and drove off. With tears of relief, I picked up the tin, held it to my chest and began the painful walk down the street. Then the battle in my mind began. What had happened to me? Would my parents believe me? Would this man really deny he did this despicable thing to me? Would my parents believe his word over mine? I sat down on the side of the road to get myself together and think about that. I came to the conclusion that I couldn't put my mother in danger of being hurt by that man. With that realization, I believed my only choice was to remain silent. I wiped my eyes, straightened my clothing and went home.

When my mother asked me if I was okay I realised I still looked a little dishevelled. I told her I had slipped over in the grass on the side of the road and explained at length how rude some people were while I was collecting. She seemed satisfied with my response and nothing more was said.

Alone in my bedroom the full impact of what had happened hit me and the pain reminded me that all was not well in my body. I began to think I must be a bad person for this terrible thing to have happened to me - whatever this terrible thing was. I felt dirty with a sense of guilt and shame and an incredible fear arose inside of me. Where was God? Wasn't He supposed to prevent such things happening to good girls? I felt like He had let me down. At that time I knew *about* God, because my family attended Church regularly, but I did not really *know* Him.

Even though excessive showering became a lifestyle, the feeling of uncleanness would not leave me. My emotions were out of control and I didn't recognize the person I had become. I joined with a group of girls at school who were heavily into sexual activities – a group the other girls avoided due to their loose characters. I learned from their conversations that what I had experienced was rape – yet I never shared my experience with them. I was being drawn to those whom I formally judged and despised for their bad reputation. I began to want to do the things they did even though the thought of what had happened to me still haunted and revolted me. What were these weird feelings I felt as they talked about their sexual encounters? What was the matter with me – was I going insane?

My concerned mother was constantly asking me if there was anything wrong and I would reassure her that everything was okay. Carrying this secret pain and not knowing how to deal with these new, indescribable emotions and uncontrollable desires drove me into a lifestyle I could never have imagined possible. I was a preacher's daughter who professed to be a Christian even though I didn't yet have a personal relationship with God. How many times my dad must have asked himself, 'What has happened to my darling daughter?'

Prior to this assault at the age of 14, I was a quiet, shy person who enjoyed my own company. I didn't make friends very easily or show much emotion. But I was obedient to my parents and those in authority over me. I did what was right and what was expected of me. I was honest and knew who I was - a 'good girl' because I knew God as One who sat in Heaven with a ruler in His hand waiting to smack my knuckles if I did the wrong thing.

But the trauma of the rape sent me spiralling into the darkness of sexual sin. Suddenly my personality had completely changed. I was loud, resisted all attempts to 'control' me and was totally rebellious. Even worse I had this insatiable desire for sex. It was a driving force within me that only the sexual act could satisfy, but only temporarily. I was being drawn into a pathway of destructive sexual relationships and I began to see everything in life through distorted glasses.

I hated what I had become and the lifestyle I was leading. I would commit sexual sin, and then lie in my bed at night crying; wondering what on earth was wrong with me. What was driving me? Was I totally evil? Where was God? I remember saying to Him after a sexual encounter, 'I'm sorry – I'm determined I won't do it again'. But He knew I would, and I did, over and over again. I kept spiralling downhill.

My life was dominated by fear and my mind was in torment. I felt as though I was in prison, unable to trust anybody. My anger became so explosive I was a threat to myself and anybody who dared to try and control me even in the mildest way. I had been defiled and I would have murdered the rapist if I ever met him again. Shame was a heavy weight on my shoulders. It didn't matter how many times a day I showered I still felt unclean. I was out of control, hating what I had become.

I kept reliving the horror of the experience so that there was no escape from the images in my mind. Such was my despair I even tried to commit suicide. I felt my life was ruined and nothing would ever change. Hopelessness was like a black cloud hanging over me. As I became entangled one by one in these destructive forces, the darkness distorted everything I saw and thought.

My father did not know how to handle this deterioration in my behaviour and lifestyle. He was totally ashamed of what I had become. When he began to withdraw from me and favour my older sister and younger brother, I knew that I was just bad, very bad. I knew my mother still loved me even though she could not understand what I had become. I felt like an outcast, even in my own family.

The answer my dad finally came up with was to send me to a psychologist to have me assessed. Because of the threats made by the rapist I chose not to reveal anything to the psychologist even though he told me what I shared was strictly confidential. Although part of me wanted to spill out the whole story and put an end to the torment, I was too afraid of not being believed and of possible hurt to my mother.

After consultation with the psychologist my parents decided I should be admitted to hospital to receive shock treatment. Despite my denials the psychiatrist was convinced something *had* happened to me, and the memory of it needed to be removed so that I could resume a normal life. It was easier for my dad to tell others that I had a mental illness than to admit that his lovely daughter had become a bad girl.

So I was admitted to a small private hospital and shock treatment was administered over several weeks. That in itself was another horror, the worst part being that nothing changed! When I was released my life of promiscuity continued but now I had the added label of mental illness - a 'nut case' according to some local kids.

Who was the person I had become? My body, mind and emotions were badly affected. Everything about the old me had changed, even my handwriting. I was now rebellious, disobedient, loud, angry, and I certainly ran with the wrong crowd. I was known by boys as an easy girl to get into bed. Promiscuity was leading me on a journey of self-destruction which was to continue for many years.

I was desperately unhappy. Self-hatred dominated my life and I had lost all hope of life ever returning to what I knew as normal before I was raped. Keeping that experience to myself was an intolerable torment. On the rare occasion when I considered telling my mother, I remembered the threat from the rapist. Even though it was incredibly difficult to watch her suffer on account of my lifestyle change, the thought of the rapist doing something to hurt her kept my lips firmly sealed.

Listening to others who had similar experiences and were now living a lifestyle much like mine, I learned that you can develop an exterior personality which was attractive to the outside world while keeping the trauma and pain hidden within. I became very practiced at being the life of the party wherever I went. A talent for humour enabled me to entertain others and keep them laughing, but hidden inside was this little child crying all day in unbelievable pain.

I married at the age of nineteen to the first man who didn't want sex on our first date. I decided he was a decent boy who wouldn't just use my body. Lyall was the first person who had ever proposed to me. I knew nobody else ever would, so I accepted. Even when my father insisted that I tell him of my lifestyle he still wanted to marry me. I was foolish enough to believe that marriage, with a licence to have sex whenever I felt like it, would fix everything. Wrong! It became obvious my husband was not very interested in the sexual side of marriage. However, within sixteen months I became pregnant to him and gave birth to a beautiful daughter, Cheryl. At last I had somebody to love who would love me back. I absolutely adored her and she brought so much pleasure. For her sake I vowed to change my ways for the better.

But my husband's declining sexual interest drew me back into the old habits of sleeping around. I realised that nothing had changed, except that now I wore a wedding ring. My sexual sin was now adultery. My emotions were so screwed up. I could not understand why this sexual drive was impossible to restrain. Even the love for my darling daughter could not stop the compulsive promiscuity.

Eventually I became pregnant to another man. I knew it was not my husband's child because we had not slept together for so long. I knew I could get him to have sex with me and then tell him it was his baby, but sexual promiscuity hadn't destroyed my basic honesty. I believed in telling the truth despite the fact that I was already living outer and inner lives that didn't match.

In spite of Lyall's mother begging him to allow me to keep the baby, he insisted I give him up for adoption. After a very difficult pregnancy and birth, it broke my heart to hand my beautiful baby over. Despite not having a good relationship with God I remember praying and asking Him to ensure the child was raised in a Christian home by parents who really loved Him.

Following this heartache, I was diagnosed with a serious kidney condition. I had a number of major surgeries, including the removal of one of my kidneys. I was told I would not survive another pregnancy. However, with Lyall's encouragement, I went back to the obstetrician to explore the possibility of another child. We were told that a baby might survive but my chance was minimal. Nevertheless, I felt obligated to try again for Lyall's sake.

Heartbreak knocked on my door again just two years later in 1970. In the midst of sickness and the continuation of my promiscuous lifestyle I became pregnant again. This time I knew it was my husband's baby because I had taken precautions with other men. Both Lyall and I were elated and drawn closer by the birth of our beautiful baby boy. At last a brother, Robert James, for our daughter and another child for us to love.

I had fed him for only two days when hospital staff observed that he was not breathing properly. He was rushed to the Children's' Hospital by ambulance. My husband went with him. My beautiful baby boy underwent emergency heart surgery but died the next day. I was devastated. Around and around went my thoughts: I deserve this, but it's not fair that my husband and daughter suffer, too. Was I so evil that nothing good could come out of my life? It's uncanny that he died from a malformed heart when my own heart was broken into many pieces.

My husband insisted we adopt a child, despite my parents' opposition because of my failing health. Encouraged by the obstetrician, we proceeded down that path and a few weeks later we were called to a hospital to collect a two week old baby, David. I could not get my head around that. It was only a few weeks since we had buried our son. My husband and daughter were overjoyed, but I looked at the baby placed in my arms and didn't know how I would cope. But when I acknowledged the joy he gave to Lyall and Cheryl, I just put on another mask – the doting mother – and accepted him into our home. From that moment, my husband's attention was focused on his son. Cheryl and I took a back seat while baby David got all his time and love.

My sister in law literally took over David's upbringing during the day. Apart from being in poor health, I was still grieving for my dead baby. I simply could not transfer that love to David, but I knew he needed to be loved by someone while Lyall was at work. No need to guess what happened next! I went back into the old lifestyle, despite my health issues.

My health had improved by the time Cheryl began school and I considered looking for a job. I hadn't worked since before she was born so I was unsure what employment might be available to me. I was in for a surprise. One of my friends was also looking for employment so each day we purchased *The Advertiser* and enjoyed a coffee together as we trawled the situations vacant. One morning there was an advertisement for a Secretarial Teacher in a Business College. When she dared me to apply, I did, just for a joke.

It was a shock when the owners of the College telephoned me and offered an interview. I had good references from past employment but the interview was intense. At the end of it I was convinced I wouldn't even be considered. A week later I was invited to a second interview. After another nerve-wracking, drawn-out session I was asked to wait outside while they discussed my application. When they called me back into the office they explained that they were not only looking for a teacher but also a new Principal. I was offered the College Principal position.

I excelled in that position for several years before I resigned due to a return of ill health. Later, when my health improved , I returned to the workforce as the Principal of the Reception Centre in Adelaide. Once again, my health declined and this time I was forced to remain at home.

Finally I left my marriage and went with the man with whom I was currently having an affair. That relationship ended when he began having affairs. Now I knew what it was to be on the other end of the stick.

I jumped straight from that disappointment into a second de facto relationship which also ended in disaster. I didn't want to lose the nice home I had built with that man so I went to my ex-husband and talked him into having another shot at our marriage. He bought the other man out and we were back together as a family. But even though we remarried, nothing else had changed. It was a shame because Lyall was a good man. He was a hard worker, provided well for the family and had extremely good morals. But he really didn't know how to demonstrate love. That was not his fault. He was brought up in a family who were unable to demonstrate love to one another. What I needed in my broken, messed up life was to know and be shown that I was loved. Even just telling me that he loved me would have made a huge difference, but even that he could not do.

After we remarried, I managed to hold a part time position in the office at the local High School, and later, after the removal of one of my kidneys, my health improved sufficiently for me to return to teaching at the business college. But once again my health deteriorated and I was back in hospital. This time the prognosis was devastating. I was still in my twenties and the doctors were telling me I would not live to be 30 years old. Two years was all I would get. I didn't really care for myself – I hated myself - but I did have a much loved daughter and I was crushed to think I wouldn't be there for her.

In those years of sickness, I had some good neighbours. They brought meals when I was so ill. The problem was they were Christians and talked to me about God all the time and gave me a Bible to read. I didn't mind the meals, but all the God talk? What had God done to help me with my life?

Chapter 2
EXPERIENCING HEAVEN

In 1978 I was in Intensive Care at the Royal Adelaide Hospital. I had chronic kidney problems and was experiencing severe pain. Suddenly I began feeling lighter and lighter until I felt weightless. When I registered that the shocking pain was no longer present I realised I was floating upwards. I looked down at my body lying on the bed below me. There was no fear, just perfect peace.

As I rose higher I could clearly see the helicopter pad on the roof of the hospital. I felt fresh, outside air upon my body. Even though it was dark there seemed to be a pathway which was full of light. I was travelling fast but I had complete peace and I had no pain or discomfort. I didn't feel nauseous, my ears weren't popping and I wasn't worried or concerned, but I did wonder what was happening to me. I wondered where I was going and what would happen next. Even as I asked these questions, I noticed that I was being carried by a beautiful angel dressed in white. The angel seemed delighted to be carrying me upwards.

As we approached a magnificent, golden Heavenly city we began to slow down. As we came nearer, gates of pearl opened and there was the city with its golden streets. Angels in white, carrying swords, guarded the gate but they granted us access into Heaven. There were angels everywhere. Angels talking, angels singing, angels playing musical instruments, angels dancing and praising their King! I was surrounded by the most beautiful singing. Angels were singing to the Lord Jesus. You've never heard singing until you hear a multitude of angels singing praise. I have difficulty finding words to describe it.

The light was the purest I had ever seen and the music was glorious and in perfect timing. I was overwhelmed by its beauty and holiness. I felt that this was where I belonged and I didn't want to leave.

Suddenly Jesus appeared, moving toward me. He wore a beautiful white robe with a solid gold belt around His waist. His blue eyes were deep pools of love. A radiant light came from Him. When Jesus looked at me, His eyes pierced me with pure love. He is more beautiful, wonderful and glorious than I can put into words. I was seeing Jesus, and I was part of Jesus – I was in Him.

Then I noticed He was holding the hand of a young boy. Jesus greeted me and then said 'Lee, this is your son, Bobbie.' I was stunned. I had lost my beautiful baby son when he was three days old and I had expected to see him just like that again when I passed into Heaven. I had named him Robert James, but I was willing to accept that Jesus called him, Bobbie.

Jesus looked down at Bobbie and asked, 'Would you like to show Mama around?' 'Yes, I would,' Bobbie replied. With a smile, Jesus began to walk away, leaving Bobbie and me together. 'I will come back for you when it is time to say goodbye.'

As we walked hand in hand I said, 'Bobbie, I am sorry I didn't recognize you. I was so surprised to find you had grown, I thought you would still be a little baby.' 'Oh no Mama' Bobbie replied, 'There is no death here. Heaven is filled with life. Even those who die in their Mama's tummy come here and live. There is so much love, grace and mercy here, Mama, but no sickness, pain, sorrow or tears. Let me show you some of my favourite places.'

Bobbie shared with me how he loved life in Heaven. He loved the magnificent, rainbow colours that permeated the heavens. He was loved and cared for by angels as well as adults who now lived here and had so much to share.

We wandered around admiring the beauty of nature. I noticed I was walking on a lush, green carpet of grass but there were no indentations where I had stepped. It was perfect. Not a bent blade, nothing out of place. Nothing is harmed in heaven. The grass was the most vivid green I have ever seen. It stretched over hills that were sprinkled with all types and colours of flowers. They were so vibrantly alive, it was as though they, too, were praising God.

The landscaped grounds were filled with huge trees and they were so, so tall. One in particular caught my attention because it seemed to be so wide. The leaves were shaped like teardrops and made a continual sound of chimes as they brushed against each other. This tree glowed with light and sound. It was aflame with glory from top to bottom. There were also fruit trees. I picked a piece of fruit from one and immediately another piece grew in its place. The fruit tasted absolutely gorgeous.

There were flowers of every imaginable size and colour and they were so bright. I saw roses that were huge. The flowers faced me and they were all humming. The air was filled with their aroma. All the plant life was amazing in its beauty and there were no spent flowers; nothing dying, everything alive. The fragrance of Heaven was gentle and sweet.

At the end of one of the streets there was a small water fountain. The jet sprays were perfectly angled so that the water spouted up in perfect symmetry. There was a perfectly clear river, delightful waterfalls and majestic mountains. It was beautiful beyond belief and filled with joy and overwhelming peace.

There was a great deal of light everywhere and I knew it was the glory of God. I was so conscious that I was in a place with the real and living God. Every song, poem, dance was directed to God in worship. There is total love, total peace and everything is perfect. There is no fear in Heaven. Everything and everyone expressed their love to God in different ways.

The angels kept singing and as they did the trees clapped and kept rhythm to their singing. Everything worships God in Heaven. Flowers had faces and they sang. It was amazing!

Bobbie took me to Heaven's nursery. It was filled with love. Special attention was given to those babies who came to Heaven from their Mama's wombs even before they were born. There were babies who had died in the womb (miscarriages) or died in infancy, and there were aborted babies, all of them completely happy and free. The children forgive their parents, and they want their parents to forgive themselves. The children would be hurt to know that their parents continue to carry guilt all their lives. All the children were extremely warm and loving. No matter what the cause of death, they were all loved to life.

Heaven's Kindergarten was the next stop and it was a place filled with fun and laughter. The teachers who now lived in Heaven worked with the angels to care for Bobbie and other children, teaching them the things they needed to learn. I could see Bobbie was growing into a beautiful young boy.

Then we visited the Schools in Heaven. They were such happy places. There was real pleasure in learning and it was sheer joy just being with the other children of every age and every race. Bobbie loved growing up in Heaven with all the other children and angels as his friends and playmates. Jesus Himself was his most treasured Friend.

Bobbie shared with me that Jesus regularly spent time with him. Bobbie loved the variety of things they enjoyed together. Sometimes they just spent time talking and laughing. Other times they walked together in the garden, rested alongside the beautiful river, or ran and played together on the mountains. His favourite times were when everybody gathered together to worship God before the throne. 'How privileged I am to experience the love of the Heavenly Father watching over me while I gaze in awe and wonder upon His majesty, His glory, His power and His holiness'.

I had a foretaste of the great city of the King, the city of God where all things are made new. I would like to write more but I cannot. It is difficult to describe Heaven with earthly words. There are limitations to what we can put into writing. Such things can only be known by experiencing Heaven for yourself, or directly through the revelation of Holy Spirit.

After a wonderful time together touring the gardens of Heaven and the places where children were the central focus, Jesus returned to us. His love is so tangible. It is in a dimension different from our idea of love. With such an expression of love and a huge smile He said, 'Lee, you must go back now. It is not your time yet. Please tell My children I love them – yes I really, really love them. And let Bobbie's daddy and the rest of the family know they need to keep on following Me'.

'Yes,' added Bobbie, 'and tell them that I love them very much and I will be waiting at the gate ready to celebrate with them when they come'. Bobbie hugged me. 'Bye, Mama, it was so lovely to see you. I'll be watching and waiting for your return'. Instantly I was back in my body and there was that devastating pain again.

After several days I had improved enough to be taken from intensive care back to the Renal Unit. As I was wheeled along the corridor I noticed the staff were staring at me in disbelief. It was obvious when I reached my room that all my possessions had been removed. When they were eventually returned to me I understood they had been packed to send home because I was not expected to live. Ten days later I was well enough to be discharged. I went home to recover from my ordeal and learn to live with an incurable kidney condition.

However, I could not get my mind off my encounter with Heaven. It consumed me day and night. I knew now that Jesus Christ was real and so was life after death. When my next door neighbours dropped in to visit me I was far more interested in what they had to share about a new life in Christ. I listened as they explained what Jesus did on the Cross of Calvary. He didn't just die to take the penalty for my sin, but also so that I could be healed from my sickness and disease. That certainly got my attention. I also understood that I could enjoy a personal relationship with Jesus Christ. I could talk to Him and He would answer me. Wow!

But my acceptance of the gospel of Jesus Christ was only partial. I liked the idea of being healed, so I accepted that part: that Jesus Christ was my Healer. Because of God's great grace and mercy He honoured even my partial acceptance of Him and when I agreed to be prayed for, I was instantly and completely healed – at least for the time being.

After my physical healing I began to pursue Jesus Christ and very soon I noticed that my fear had left. In its place was a tremendous peace. I was seeing things more clearly, but I still had a broken heart. I still hated myself. I was always drawn to bad company – doing bad things.

I decided to do as my neighbours suggested and began to read the Bible. There was much I didn't understand, but I did find some verses that made me think a lot. I would like to share just a few:

Psalm 147:3
'He heals the broken-hearted and binds up their wounds'.

I wondered if this Jesus could heal my heart. It seemed to be broken in so many pieces. When I finally came to the place where I gave Him all the broken pieces, He did heal my heart.

Isaiah 53:3-5 (talking about Jesus on the Cross)
*'He was despised and rejected, a Man who suffered,
Who knew pain first hand. One look at Him
and the people turned away.
They looked down on Him and thought He was
worthless – of no value.
But the fact is, it was our pains He carried
our disfigurements, all the things wrong with us.
We thought He brought it on Himself – that God was
punishing Him for His own failures, but it was our sins that
did that to Him - that ripped at Him, that tore at Him
and crushed Him – our sins!
He took the punishment, and that made us whole.
Through His bruises we get healed!*

I suddenly saw from these verses that Jesus died not only so I could be healed, but I could also be forgiven for all my sins (and there were plenty of them). I began to understand how much God loved me, if he would allow Jesus to go through all that suffering for me and for other sinners like me.

Luke 5:32 (Jesus said)
'I have not come to call the righteous, but the sinners, to repentance'

I asked Jesus to forgive me for all the things I'd done wrong, then I asked Him to come into my heart and to be Lord of my life (seeing I had made a complete mess of it!) To my surprise, when I did that, it was as if a great heaviness was lifted off. I encountered the love of God – the light of Jesus came into my darkness and my despair lifted from me.

1 John 1:9:
'If we confess our sins, He is faithful and just to forgive us our sins and to cleanse us from all unrighteousness'.

Did you hear that? I was not only forgiven, but cleaned from defilement of the rape! I felt clean and pure for the first time since the rape, 20 years earlier.

Romans 5: 18,19:
'Through Jesus' righteousness the free gift came to all of us and by His obedience many will be made righteous'

The heavy cloak of shame was removed and Jesus covered me with a garment of righteousness.

I started working on getting rid of my self-hatred. I was eventually able to forgive myself and even like myself, but for now the way I saw things was becoming clearer. Hope began to rise that I could get rid of the 'bad girl' reputation I had earned for myself.

Slowly I began to trust again – that was a huge step for me. My clouded perspective was clearing, so that things were not so dark any more, but I was still a very angry person and still tormented in my mind.

Psalm 23:1-3
'The Lord is my Shepherd, I shall not want
He makes me to lie down in green pastures (rest)
He leads me beside still waters (peace)
He restores my soul (mind, will and emotions)
He leads me in the paths of righteousness
for His name sake'

So I asked God to help me get rid of my anger and the mental torment. There is a story in Matthew chapter 18 about a man who was forgiven a large debt which he couldn't repay. But despite that he insisted on payment of a debt that was owed to him and became angry with the person when he couldn't pay. Then in verses 34 and 35 we read, if we don't forgive those who owe us (those who have hurt us or broken our hearts), we will be handed over to the tormentors.

Hang on! Now I had a dilemma! I didn't want to forgive the rapist – no, I still wanted to kill him! But did I want to spend the rest of my life angry and tormented in my mind? The rapist didn't deserve my forgiveness – I didn't deserve God's either! I suddenly realised that my unforgiveness had absolutely no effect on the rapist; it was only causing *me* mental torment.

I made the choice to forgive and the torment stopped. It was not easy for me. I did not want to forgive him, so I needed God's help. Every morning for six weeks I said 'Heavenly Father, I choose to forgive the rapist. Would you please help me to make that a reality in my life'? On that last morning it was like my insides exploded and the unforgiveness was completely gone. Over time my anger disappeared, too. God removed my 'glasses' of distortion completely. I see clearly now. I no longer want to take my own life. I am off the pathway of self-destruction. I have such joy. I live with a purpose and a sense of destiny.

I give God all the praise because I have discovered what God says in His Word, the Holy Bible, is absolutely true. Jesus Christ found me in a trash heap; picked me up and made me His own special treasure.

However, even after getting my life together following my Heavenly encounter and physical healing, I realised I still had that overwhelming desire for sex. I was still driven by lust. It was a shocking blow to discover that I was not free in that area of my life even when other areas had changed. I soon found myself sleeping around again as I was never sexually satisfied within my marriage.

A few short years into our re-marriage we realised our relationship was disintegrating again. We decided it would never work for us and that it was time to separate. This time we chose to talk with each of the children separately and let them decide who they wanted to live with. I thought that was a great idea because I was so sure that my beloved daughter would choose to live with me, which meant we would stay in the house because of her schooling and Lyall and David would find a flat to live in. To my absolute dismay both of the children chose to live with their dad because he allowed them to do exactly as they pleased. Once again, I was in that place of devastation and heartbreak. I moved into a flat in North Adelaide, leaving behind my most treasured possession – my daughter.

My life went into a dramatic downhill spiral. Despite being physically unwell, I was still sleeping around, and barely able to earn a living. I thank God that my mother continued to love me unconditionally and helped me in every possible way.

Chapter 3
FINDING REAL LOVE

One afternoon when I was extremely lonely and depressed, I went to the local hotel. I had never been a drinker so I didn't even know what to order. I finally decided on a red wine. I almost choked on my first mouthful, but decided it would eventually make me feel better because that's what my drinking friends had been telling me for years. But before I could take my next sip a voice behind me said 'What are you doing in here? Thinking it was one of my friends who knew I didn't drink, I turned around, but there was nobody there. I picked up the glass for another sip, and the voice spoke again 'What is My daughter doing in here?' This time I didn't have to turn around to know it was Father God speaking to me. I went home. At this lowest time of my life I knew God still cared for me and was saving me from going down a path I could have lived to regret.

During my re-marriage to Lyall and before my health began to deteriorate I was working at a local High School. I became friendly with Av, and before long she and her husband, Alan, Lyall and myself were spending some evenings together. We discovered that Av's and Lyall's birthdays were only a few days apart and Alan's and mine were too, so for some years we did something special together on those two occasions.

After I had moved into the flat in North Adelaide I learned that Av had asked Alan to leave their home as she wanted a male friend to move in. My heart broke for him. I knew what that felt like! I wanted to contact him but decided that would not be the right thing to do even if I had felt well enough to make the effort. In fact it was not long after this that I was flown to Melbourne for life-saving surgery and treatment. It came at such a low point in my life that I rather hoped it would not be successful. My life was not worth living.

It was while I was recovering in the Melbourne Hospital that Alan phoned me to ask how I was. During our chat he shared what had been happening in his life, too. It seemed that we were both in a very low period of our lives.

After returning to Adelaide I received another phone call from Alan reminding me it was both our birthdays and inviting me to have dinner with him as we used to do as a foursome. I couldn't see any harm in it, so I accepted. We both needed some cheering up.

Alan took me to a great restaurant. We shared our stories of marriage breakup and how it affected us. After a beautiful meal we danced together and it seemed as though we just danced the blues away. What a wonderful evening it turned out to be! Several weeks later Alan contacted me again to invite me out. I was so pleased because that first evening together had been so enjoyable and lifted my spirit.

We were so alike in many ways and really enjoyed each other's company so we began dating regularly. I had never felt so free in my life – free to be myself and accepted as I am. I was beginning to feel loved and appreciated for the first time in my life. But all the time I was so scared Alan would find out the sort of person I really was. Yes, I was a successful school teacher at Muirden College and appeared to be a lady who had it all together. I was this fun-loving Christian with an amazing sense of humour, enjoying life to the fullest, but inside was the girl who hated herself, despised what she had become, and was not worthy to receive love, kindness or anything good. I knew that although I enjoyed this wonderful new relationship I still struggled with lust. There was a difference, however. Though lust tormented me, I wasn't sleeping around. I am sure this was because I felt so loved and accepted by Alan and I didn't want to do anything to hurt him.

Alan enjoyed life, was morally good and a hard worker. I discovered he was so genuine both inside and out: someone who deserved the best out of life, not what his wife had done to him. He spoke in a broad English accent and at times I found it difficult to understand what he was saying. I felt awkward to ask him to explain. Av, his first wife, was also English but had immigrated to Australia when they were newly married. I knew he hadn't needed to repeat things to her over and over again. But he was so gracious and tolerant with me. He never become exasperated with my 'what was that again' Thinking it must be frustrating for him, I just tried to work out what he said rather than ask.

So, after a year of dating we were enjoying a lovely evening when he said something I didn't understand. I was just happy to say 'yes' whatever the question. I decided I'd given the right answer when his eyes lit up and he kissed me passionately. Several weeks later he asked me when I wanted to get married. I replied 'You haven't asked me yet'. He explained that he proposed the last time we were out to dinner which explained why he was so happy with my answer to the question I hadn't understood!

I explained to him that as a Christian it is far better to marry somebody who has a Christian belief than someone who doesn't. He replied, 'I know that you believe in God and so do I, but there is more than that to becoming a Christian I'm sure. I have watched your life and know that there is something special inside of you'. I was encouraged that he had seen the good and not the bad. He asked me to explain what I believed in my heart about God and what effect He had on my life. I was able to share that I used to think God was a harsh task master and how the talks with my neighbours had given me a different perspective. I also shared the experience of being taken into Heaven which opened my eyes to who God really was and His love toward me. I told Alan that when I returned from Heaven I gave God control of my life.

Alan asked me what he had to do to become a Christian. I explained that in prayer he should repent of his sin and invite Jesus to come into his heart to become the Lord of his life. His response was that he wanted to do that. 'I want to do that, right now,' and immediately he knelt down and began to pray. I looked at him with amazement. Here was a man who had never been to Church, praying to ask Jesus to come into his heart and be His Lord. I knew I was seeing such absolute sincerity and reality.

Several weeks later he asked me once again when we should plan to get married. 'Oh, my gosh' I thought to myself, 'if I am ever going to marry him, I must tell him the whole truth about my life – he's seen the godly side, but hasn't got a clue about the dark side of me.' I told him I would give it some thought and let him know soon. I was devastated because I knew as soon as I told him the truth it would be the end of our wonderful friendship. Alan was so honest and faithful that I did not have the heart to deceive him. It would have to be the whole truth and no more living a lie.

For three weeks I lived in torment of the mind. Alan was such a delightful person and I was sure that he wouldn't want anything to do with the hurt and broken person that was me on the inside. What would be his reaction when the life covered with humour and fun was unwrapped and the junk was exposed? Finally, I knew it was time to let the truth be told.

After enjoying a wonderful dinner together I suggested we go back to my flat for coffee instead of having it at the restaurant. My heart sank further and further the closer we came to my flat. We sat down together with our coffee and I said 'It is time for me to give you an answer to your proposal of marriage.' His face lit up and I knew he was expecting me to say 'Yes.' I began by telling him that I was unable to answer until I disclosed the real me to him. He looked a little confused but didn't say anything. I went back to the time I was raped at 14 and how my life from then on was affected by that. I told him that what he knew of me was a mask hiding the person I had become following my rape. I went into great detail, even to the point of explaining that I still struggled with lust even though I had not given in to that disgusting impulse since we had been dating. When I looked up at him there were tears in his eyes. All I could think was, 'This dear beautiful man, having to hear all this. He is genuinely upset that I am not who he thought I was'.

When I had finished telling him all there was to tell, he put his arm around me, kissed me and looked right into my eyes. 'Thank you so much for your complete honesty. I realise how difficult that must have been for you. I love you even more for that and I still want us to get married. I will do all I can to stand with you as we work through this together.' I was not sure what that meant, but my heart leapt for joy. I replied, 'I love you too and my answer is yes, I would be very honoured to become your wife'. News of our engagement travelled around fast as Alan simply couldn't contain his joy. It was healing to my soul to know that somebody loved me so much he was willing to overlook my gruesome past to take me as his wife.

In November of 1982 we had the most amazing wedding day. I would have to say it was the best day of my life. I was marrying the only person in all of my life, who not only said he loved me but was able to demonstrate it in so many wonderful ways. I felt like a thoroughly spoiled child and I loved it!

My ex-husband, Lyall, had sold our family home and purchased a smaller one, so I received my share from the sale. When Alan's wife, Av, sold theirs and moved down south with her new friend, Alan had his share too. This enabled us to purchase our own home. What a sense of joy and excitement as we moved in, did some renovations and made it our own.

It was a new beginning for both of us. Our marriage felt like it was made in Heaven. I was so happy I often felt I was in a beautiful dream more than reality. I was so blessed by God to have such a loving, caring husband.

Less than a year later Alan came home from work to break the news to me that the business he was working for had gone bankrupt and was going into receivership. He no longer had a job. I had never seen him so downcast. It was a terrible blow because we had taken out a bank loan and purchased our home on the basis of having two incomes. Alan immediately began looking for another job, but after months of interviews we realised we were in trouble financially and could lose our home.

Because I knew many teachers in state schools I began asking a few questions and discovered that those teaching in country areas not only received more income, but they could also rent houses very reasonably. Alan and I discussed the pros and cons and I made an appointment with the Education Department. The interview was positive and I made myself available should any country position in the field I taught in become available. It was difficult for Alan and me to contemplate moving to the country, but we considered it would only be temporary and prevent the loss of our home. There was another issue: Cheryl was now living with us because it had not worked out for her living with her father and brother. We shared our predicament with my mother who agreed to have Cheryl move in with her if we had to make the move to the country.

I was offered a position at Booleroo Centre High School. It was a town we had never heard of despite it being close to Melrose, which was a popular tourist area. We made the three hour trip to check out the town and surrounding areas. Booleroo Centre was certainly off the beaten track! But we spoke with several residents and found a friendliness that was encouraging. There was still no work for Alan so the choice was either a year or two in the country or lose our home by March. I accepted the teaching position.

We had about six weeks to place our home with a rental agent and pack up. Many decisions had to be made - what to take and what to leave. We had not seen the house we were to rent in nearby Murray Town, close to Booleroo Centre. How big was it? How small? What were the essentials? What could we live without? And all that paperwork – the number of people we had to notify and bills to finalize! In the midst of the chaos the agent was bringing people through our home who were interested in renting in our area. We were pleased with the Air Force family who eventually moved in. There was Cheryl's relocation that had to be organised, too, but fortunately my mother's home was only 15 minutes away. And in the midst of all this there was Christmas! It was disorganised but we made sure it was enjoyable.

As the removal van pulled into the driveway, reality hit. Had we done the right thing? Was there really no other way? It was an emotional morning. The Rental Property Agent arrived to collect the keys and finalise arrangements. Our next house payment was due in a fortnight and he asked for the money. When we told him we didn't have it he was shocked, but agreed to take it out of the first rent received. He proved to be an excellent agent.

The semi left and we had to say our goodbyes. Cheryl and I were in tears – we wouldn't see each other for a month - but Alan and I had agreed to come back to Adelaide one weekend every month to catch up with family and friends. So our new adventure began. Finally, we were on our way to Booleroo Centre to experience an entirely different way of life.

Having collected the keys to the Education Department home we were to rent we were astonished to discover just how small it was. It was a challenge to fit in all our furniture, but with our own things around us it soon began to feel like home.

We had several days to settle in and become familiar with the town and the route from Murray Town to Booleroo Centre. We soon realised that school teachers from the city were given the utmost respect - something that was rare in the city and suburbs. We were overwhelmed by the hospitality of the locals. People dropped in to introduce themselves and invited us into their homes. This attention was new to us, but it was normal culture in the country. We were made to feel welcome and accepted.

Two days after our arrival, we attended the Uniting Church just across the road from our home. It seemed strange to simply walk a few steps to attend Church. Quite a fuss was made of us as we were welcomed into the Church. We had never felt so honoured and yes, it felt so good. It confirmed that we had made the right decision in coming to the country for a season.

During the same week I attended the school preparation days, getting to know the other teachers, planning schedules, making rosters etc. I discovered I was not the only new person teaching years 11 and 12 and a couple of them were also from Adelaide. We were all amazed at our acceptance by country teachers. It was a wonderful time of establishing friendships and bonding together as a team to ensure everything was in place for the students to begin the following week. An excitement began to rise within me as I anticipated the beginning of a new era, not only as a country school teacher but also living in a close knit community.

Chapter 4
LIFE IN THE COUNTRY

As I awoke on to that first day of school in the country I admit I felt nervous. But on arrival I was greeted as if I had lived there all of my life and had just come back from school holidays. The staff were like best friends, willing to explain protocols and offer help where needed. But what impressed me the most was that students were so well behaved, obedient to instruction and worked studiously all day. Compared to those in the city it was almost too good to be true. I wondered if they were only trying to create a good impression on my first day, but to my delight it proved to be their normal enthusiasm and desire to achieve.

The adjustment from city to country was so easy it felt like we had lived there all our lives. Alan fitted in extremely well, too, and farmers were offering him casual farm work. As they observed his good work ethic, word travelled fast and he was soon fully employed. Country hospitality is wonderful. We were being invited to other folk's homes for dinners or lunches on the weekend. It was so wonderful to know that people just wanted to spend time together with us to get to know us.

Except for the weekend we went back to the city, Alan and I attended the Uniting Church across the road from our home. When the Minister learned that I used to lead home groups in the city I was asked to begin a group in our home. It was very encouraging to us that the group continued to grow in numbers and spiritually.

In the country leaders are not confined to one Church but minister in several others in the area. Because of this each of the Churches was closed once a month. We began to notice that people often turned up and were disappointed not having realised it was the off-Sunday. When I mentioned this to the Minister, he said there didn't have to be an off-Sunday. 'Now that you are here you can lead the service on that day!' I had never preached in my life, but he told me it was not much different from teaching and he had great faith that I would do an excellent job. So I accepted the challenge. And a challenge it was!

One of the things about living in the country is that your whole life is soon 'all in together' in one box. What I mean by that is that in the city you have your school life in one 'box', your social life in another and yet another for your Church life and Christian friends. Little did we know when we left Adelaide that country life is 'all in together'.

Initially, it was difficult for me to be sitting across the dinner table with friends whose child was in one of my classes. I struggled even more to see students in the congregation on the weeks that I was leading the meeting and preaching the sermon. However, as time went on I realised that's how it should be. We are not three different persons engaged in three different areas of life. We are the same person. Once I had that revelation it was much easier to be 'me' in all areas.

Midway through that first year we were offered a much larger country home on a farming property nearer the school. With plenty of space and a secure yard, we purchased a Labrador puppy. He brought much pleasure to Alan, but because I was still struggling with rejection, low self esteem and the lust problem I became jealous of the dog. When Alan came home from work the dog would run through the doggy door to wait at the gate. He had all of Alan's attention even before I got a 'hello'. When we watched TV, Alan and the dog were together on the two-seater and I sat in a single lounge chair. For somebody who was screwed up on the inside that was just a slap in the face. Even though I looked like a confident, well adjusted teacher and preacher, I was still this broken, wounded, hurting person on the inside.

One of the things Alan and I laughed about for years after was the day that I tied the dog up inside the house and when I heard his car pull up I climbed through the doggy door on all fours and went down the path to the gate wagging my butt. I expected to get all the attention but all I received was outlandish laughter and not even one pat! It hurt. However, it enabled Alan and me to discuss how I felt on the inside (which was quite a shock to him) and we made some changes in our lifestyle to help me overcome some of these feelings. Nothing really changed at that time except, sad to say, that poor doggy didn't quite get as much attention as he used to.

Towards the end of that year I was driving back to Adelaide to attend a conference for year 12 teachers when I skidded on the gravel road and rolled my car several times. It rolled between two large trees and landed on its left side, some distance from the road into a paddock. The engine was still running. It seemed to take forever to free myself from the seatbelt, turn off the ignition and pull myself together. When I reached up to the driver's door to push it open, it would not budge, no matter how hard I pushed. I sat back down on what was the passenger door and realised I was in trouble. It was early morning and I was in a paddock by a little used country road. Who was going to notice what had happened? I suddenly thought, 'but God'. I rose to place my hands on the door above me and pushed once more with all my might. Still no movement. I prayed aloud: 'Lord, You see my situation, and Your Word says to trust You in every situation, so I am calling upon You to help me out of here!'

The next thing I remember I was standing on the road, with my hands still in the air, right in front of a farmhouse. I knocked on the door, and the owner emerged looking a little grumpy. I think I may have woken him up. But when I told him what had happened he woke his wife who made me some coffee while I phoned Alan to let him know what was going on. John and Mary were more than willing to help. John asked how far away the car was I told him it was just around the corner and he went off to see what he could do.

John was a long time returning and when he did he looked rather shaken. 'How far away did you say your car was?' 'Just around the corner,' I replied. He raised his eyebrows and said it was more like two and a half kilometres. He asked how I got out of the car, but all I could remember was praying and then standing on the road near his house. He went white. He told me that he had climbed onto the side of the car to open the door and after trying with all his might it would not open. He said 'How the heck did you get out of that car?' I was still in shock and I could not give him an answer.

When Alan arrived with another farmer friend, the three men went back to the rolled car while I stayed with Mary and tried to rest. Confusion had set in as an after effect of shock and I didn't know what to make of John's report. By this time I was also experiencing pain in my neck, which didn't help.

The men were gone for a long time. Each of them was unsuccessful in their attempts to open the driver's door. Lying on its side as it was, they were able to examine the underneath of the car and it was obvious to them that the chassis was twisted. There was no way that door could have been opened. So how *did* I get out? Only when they heaved the car back onto its wheels could that door be opened!

Alan took me to the doctor's rooms where I was given medication for pain. I also had an x-ray to determine the injury and my neck was placed in a brace. I was sent home to rest.

That night I tossed and turned as I relived the experience. I had already observed that the high-heeled shoes I'd been wearing showed absolutely no signs of wear from walking on a gravel road for two and a half kilometres. And there was no way somebody with my organizational personality would leave keys and handbag in the car! It had to be God Who had supernaturally removed me from the car and transported me to John and Mary's farmhouse. This realization couldn't wait til morning. I woke Alan to tell him and together we fell on our knees beside the bed and thanked God. He is a good God! We asked John and Mary around to our home for dinner soon afterwards and we shared with them what we believed. John's simple response was, 'I don't know about that, but I do know this, you didn't get out of that door'.

I was asked to start a Christian group in the school during the lunch break once a week. It started with a small number but continually increased until I had to divide it into two separate groups on two different days. Some of the students took advantage of that and attended both days, which spoke for itself. It was great to know that the students enjoyed it as much as I did - even greater that they wanted more of God.

At the end of the school year Alan and I took a holiday to England - neck brace and all - to spend some time with his parents and brother. Meeting Alan's family was really special, and it proved to be party, party, party the whole time we were there! We also went up into Scotland for a few days, alone. Altogether, it was a wonderful celebration of our first year as country folk.

The second year brought good things for Alan. When the school Groundsman went on long-service leave for four months, Alan was asked to take on that job. He loved gardening. Then one of the bus drivers retired, and Alan was asked to take on that job. The Principal had seen that he was a good and careful driver. After undergoing instructions in bus driving he went for his test and passed with flying colours. Yet another string to his country 'bow'. He was gaining a reputation as a real country 'bloke.'

About this time we realised it wasn't working out for my daughter Cheryl to live with my mother. There were no major problems between them; it was simply the age difference. Alan and I went with her to view a unit and we signed as her guarantors. Cheryl had a good job and could afford to buy it. We saw our lovely teenager change into a well organised adult. We were very proud of her. Later that year, Alan's son, Jason, lived with us and attended Booleroo Centre High School while his mother and her new husband caravanned around Australia. It was a joy to have him stay with us, and gave us many precious memories.

It was a very special year spiritually, too. By now I was preaching in the local Church and I taught others to lead the worship, do the Bible reading and lead the Communion, so that I was only responsible for the sermon. Invitations came in for us to minister in other Churches in the local circuit. One of the farmers gave his life to the Lord Jesus and over the next couple of weeks so did his wife and their three daughters. They began a weekly home group at their farm and I taught out there in the evening after school. We established a great relationship with this family and kept in touch for many years after we returned to the city.

I began visiting the nursing home across the road from the High School to spend some time with the residents who did not have a lot of outside contact. One beautiful Christian lady became a great encouragement and spiritual mentor as I journeyed through all these new country experiences. She heard the voice of God so accurately and spoke into my life in a wonderful and directive way. As we prayed together and I listened to her advice and godly instruction God directed my every step.

There was a man in a nearby town who was a heavy drinker. His wife was one of the elders at the Church and was one of the first to visit us and welcome us to the area, saying she had noticed something different about us the first day we attended church. She wanted to know what it was. We explained that it was Holy Spirit Who lived within us. This was a new concept to her, but she opened her heart and received Him and was gloriously filled with Holy Spirit. She had waited many years for her husband to give his life to the Lord Jesus. Alan and I had invited them for dinner one evening, and were enjoying general conversation over the meal, when suddenly I put down my knife and fork and told him, 'Do you know that you are going to hell?' Everybody was stunned, including me! I thought, 'Where on earth did that come from?' He put down his knife and fork and asked me what I meant by that. I shared the gospel with him and he gave his life to Jesus then and there. To this day I am still shocked that I said such a thing, but I know that it was a 'God thing'. He was a changed man from that moment, known by all as a good, godly man, not the local drunk he used to be.

The Year 12 Moderator who came from Adelaide several times a year to check the standard of our work told me she was impressed with the assignments I had prepared, and quality of my teaching and organization. She asked me to consider becoming a part-time Moderator who would be required to moderate the standard of Year 12 work in the surrounding country schools. This meant I would teach half time and Moderate half time, and would include quite a lot of travelling.

For a person with such a low self esteem, as I was, and still with a lust problem (controlled but not cured) I was shocked to even be considered. However, when Alan and I prayed about it we believed it was what I was supposed to undertake and I agreed to take it on for the following year.

I thoroughly enjoyed the challenge and began to feel capable in this new level of educating. I certainly loved the travelling from town to town, meeting many other teachers and principals. Twice a year I joined the panel of Moderators in Adelaide who determined the standard for Assignments at Year 12 level. I was honoured to be asked to continue in that role the following year. It was such an enjoyable challenge - and had the added bonus of increased salary.

Our Fourth year in the country continued to be one of valued friendships and acceptance of who we were and what we stood for. I was still happily teaching, preaching, moderating, and leading the school Christian group and home fellowship. We continued to go to Adelaide once a month. During one of these weekends in the city we attended the Paradise Assembly of God Church on the Sunday morning, where the guest speaker so impressed us we decided to attend the evening service (26 July 1987) instead of travelling back to Booleroo after lunch with the family. The worship had finished and the guest speaker, Al Fury, stood up to preach, but before he began he pointed to Alan and myself and asked us to stand. This is what he prophesied:

> *'For the Lord your God would say to you this night, you shall not fear and you shall not be afraid, for the day is soon coming when the door shall be opened, and yes, says the Lord your God, you will minister the Word that the Lord has given to you.*
>
> *Do not say to yourself 'we have no experience,' do not say to yourself 'we are not trained enough,' for the Lord God says, It is the anointing that breaks the yoke, and yes, if you go forth you shall minister the Word of God in power and in anointing. And yes, I shall put healing in your hands, says the Lord.*
>
> *And you shall minister to multitudes, and you will begin to hear the reports of tremendous miracles that I, the Lord, am doing through your ministry. Yes, even now says the Lord, I have set you aside that you would take time to study and*

to show yourself a workman approved by the Lord, rightly dividing the Word of Truth that needs not to be ashamed.

And I would say to you, stand by the staff, stay in the Word, seek My face, fast, and pray, says the Lord. And very, very soon I will spring a door open that no man can open normally, says the Lord; a door that you have not even dreamed of, or even thought of, says the Lord. But I the Lord will open it, and I shall propel you forth, and you will pronounce the Word of the Lord, and yes, My blessing shall be in your hand.'

Amen. Glory to God!

We were overwhelmed by the powerful authority of what he said. We knew God was speaking to us through this word, but we had no idea what it meant and where we were headed. As we drove back to the country that night we had a lot to talk about.

Over the next three months we prayed over that word and asked God what our next move was to be. We did not want to run ahead of Him, but neither did we want to be slow in moving with Him. Eventually we understood that God wanted us to move back to Adelaide but nothing more was revealed at that time.

Once a transfer back to Adelaide had been approved, it was gut-wrenching to say goodbye to the friends we had made in the area over four years. We moved back to our home in the suburbs at the end of the school year. It was satisfying to know we were now financially secure and that I had a teaching position at Modbury High School. Alan's employment was secure, too, being eligible for a government job in Adelaide because of his work for the Education Department in the country.

Chapter 5
FREE AT LAST!

Alan and I had taken to country life-style like ducks to water, but having lived in suburbia all our lives prior to that, I anticipated no hassles in re-adjusting to the city. I was in for a shock. After four years teaching years eleven and twelve and moderating for two, I was basically my own boss at Booleroo. My ordinary teaching role at Modbury High School was not so stimulating or satisfying. I settled in reasonably well. The school was close to home, the workload was good and I made new friends. But it was not long before the joy left and the job became a nightmare.

A male teacher on staff exhibited the same lust in him that I struggled with and there was an ungodly attraction to each other. I was so glad Alan was my husband. Because he loved me so much I was able to resist giving in to that attraction. With God's help, I was strengthened to a place of victory. In addition to that issue, one of the senior teachers seemed to have set against me from day one and made my life a misery. Eventually I found it necessary to take stress leave. Alan having found a good job almost as soon as we arrived back in the city, I was able to take leave without financial concerns.

Initially, taking that leave was an embarrassment to me, but it turned out to be an incredible blessing. I began meeting with Jan and Jenny as a prayer triplet. We began to come into a new level of prayer as we expected God to speak back to us. He took us on a journey with Him into areas we had never heard of, let alone experienced.

However, during this time the struggle with lust increased to an insane level. I was wearing a mask of being on such a spiritual journey with God, yet battling the most bizarre inner battle. So intense was this struggle, I was ready to walk away from what God was unveiling to us, as wonderful as it was. Then I saw an advertised book by Bill Subritsky called 'Demons Defeated'. My Church bookshop refused to order it because it didn't embrace teaching on the demonic, but I sourced it elsewhere, and it soon became obvious why I was so drawn to it.

My eyes were opened to a realm I hadn't heard much about before – the demonic realm. One particular chapter addressed the spirit of lust. This was the battle I had been going through for nearly twenty years. I approached my Pastors for help only to be told that Christians cannot have a demon.

I battled for months knowing I did have a demon - a spirit of lust - but I didn't want to go against what my Pastors were telling me. The demonic oppression was escalating and I was filled with fear that I would give in to it and return to my old ways. I loved my husband, but the battle was ferocious and I was weary with fighting.

It's amazing what we do in desperation. I obtained Bill Subritsky's phone number and rang him in New Zealand to explain my battle. He understood and confirmed that it was a spirit of lust from which I needed to be delivered. Bill was scheduled to speak at a Full Gospel Businessmen's Conference in Queensland just a few months later. He willingly agreed to minister to me one-on-one if I met him there. Nobody could ever convince me this was not a 'God arrangement'!

Alan took a week's holiday from work and we travelled to Queensland where we attended the Conference and met with Bill for personal ministry. He was such a gentleman, treating me with utmost respect. He explained that those who commit rape often have a spirit of lust that can be transferred to the victim. I had come to believe I was an evil person to have had this horrendous thing happen to me. What a relief to know that the secret thoughts I'd carried for the last twenty years were lies of the enemy. Bill ministered to me, during which he commanded the spirit of lust to leave and I was free at last. Praise God!

My life changed from that day. I was able to return to work, transferring to Gawler High School where I fitted in perfectly. Teaching was a pleasure once again. I was accepted, had the respect of my colleagues, and made new friends.

However, although I knew I was now free from the spirit of lust, I gradually became aware that I was not free in other areas. I realised I was still wearing a mask. I appeared to have my life together and be enjoying life, but on the inside I knew I had no self-esteem; I was always reacting with ungodly anger and fear and always looking for acceptance. The list of brokenness was long.

I earnestly prayed during this time asking for understanding of what was happening inside of me. With the lust gone, what was my problem? Some months earlier Alan had cut down to ground level a pear tree because its fruit was inedible. Now, in the middle of my calling out to God for answers, Alan asked me to come out into the garden to look at something. He showed me another pear tree growing where he had cut down the old one. And the Lord spoke into my heart, 'This is the answer you have been looking for. You need to get the roots out of your life so bad fruit doesn't grow back again.' This realization was to change our lives forever. We began to pray diligently for God to show us the root causes of my brokenness.

Soon after that revelation I had a work accident which resulted in a nasty back injury and put me on Work Cover leave. Even though the pain was shocking I had time to pray and seek God. Jan and

Jenny and I reconvened as a prayer triplet and we began to pursue root causes in our own lives.

Our loving Father showed us that as a tree which is cut down only to the bottom of the trunk (or has only some of its branches removed) will still grow again. The same was true in our lives. Just dealing with anger, fear, grief or depression, for example, at a surface level is not as effective as dealing with them at their roots. In other words, we were not uncovering the root of those problems, but were merely picking the fruit. That fruit keeps coming if we do not get to the roots. We learned that the only way to discover the roots of bad fruit in our lives is to ask Holy Spirit to reveal them to us. There is simply no other way.

Uncovering roots in my life dramatically changed me. Slowly my mask began to disintegrate and I became a real person. My healed inner person began to shine through at last. it was wonderful to be the 'real me'

The **Root of Bitterness** was one of the first to be exposed. This took root in my life because I had been unable to forgive those who ruined my life when they hurt me either physically (including the rapist) or with words. Unforgiveness held in the heart enables bitterness to take root. Some of the fruit in my life from this root of bitterness were physical infirmities, lack of faith, hindered prayers, and feeling unclean on the inside. I was tormented by the enemy because unforgiveness gave him a legal right to do so.

Another major root in my life was the **Root of Rejection.** As a child I knew that my older sister was my dad's favourite and my mum doted on my young brother. I had never felt accepted or wanted. I thought I was just one big mistake. As I learned about the root of rejection on my journey to freedom, I discovered that there were two main branches attached to the root. One was **self-rejection** and the other **fear of rejection**, resulting in lack of self esteem and outbursts of anger. One of my habits stemming from the fear of rejection was approval seeking. I always tried so hard with everything I did in order to gain approval. It started with trying to win my parents approval, but spread into every area of engagement - relationships and workplace. Fear of rejection combined with approval seeking was a prison for me, but thank God He set me free.

It is painful to be rejected because God did not create us to be rejected. He created us to be accepted, loved and valued. I believe it is one of the most subtle, yet powerful tools the enemy uses against people. Acceptance is a fundamental human need, and the desire for it is a basic human motivation. Seeds planted by the devil put down roots and grow into trees of rejection, but God says we should be trees of righteousness (Isaiah 61:3).

Whatever we are rooted in will determine the fruit in our lives. If we are rooted in thinking 'something is wrong with me' problems will begin to develop in our lives. They certainly did in me. When I began to think 'the *real* me is not acceptable I needed to produce a *pretend* me'.

Some of the causes of Rejection I have discovered are
- the manner and timing of conception
- rejected parents produce rejected children
- no affection ever showed to child
- problems caused by teachers or schoolmates
- words spoken against us

Experiences like these leave permanent wounds whether we are aware of them or not. Symptoms of rejection include a constant desire for physical love and assurance of self-worth.

Rejection whether active or passive, real or perceived, robs Jesus Christ of His rightful Lordship in our lives and keeps us held in bondage.

Jesus was rejected on our behalf **(Isaiah 53:3)** and when He endured the cross He set us free from rejection. He took our rejection and gave us His acceptance. We need to know our value is not in what somebody else *thinks* we are, but in what we *know* we are. **'I am accepted in the Beloved' (Eph 1:6).**

Another root I had to deal with in my life was **Shock and Trauma** which was the result of rape. This root can come from a bad accident, serious injury, life-threatening illness, any type of abuse (e.g. rape, physical violence), loss of a person in close relationship with us, or a threat to our personal integrity, just to mention a few.

Before the trauma my life was normal – security, love, joy, peace. After the trauma there was fear, terror, helplessness, anger, rage, devastation and a negative soul tie to the abuser. The long-term damage included grief/loss of expectations, emotional pain, rejection (including self-rejection and fear of rejection) guilt, shame and lack of trust – even in God.

Sometimes traumas are so horrific we simply cannot cope with them physically, mentally and emotionally, so we repress them, sometimes even to banishing them from our conscious mind. The pain is so intense that it is pushed deep down and stored in the subconscious, beyond conscious recall. Shock and trauma may blank out the memory, but it does not blank out the repercussions. Sometimes repressed memories of the past break through into our lives because something triggers a memory. That's when we need to receive inner healing and restoration under the anointing of Holy Spirit. Thank God He sent Jesus to set our imprisoned life free from the wounds of the past.

After I had been healed and set free from these three roots and other issues, my life was changed. There was freedom and there was peace. Other people began to comment on the change in my facial expression saying there was a glow about me. As I began to share with them what God had done in my life, many of them asked me to pray for them. As I did, their lives were changed too and they took on a similar 'glow'. Then their friends began asking what happened and the result was they began asking for prayer too. Eventually, I hardly had a spare moment. The testimonies of changed lives were amazing.

I was asking God how to handle all the people who were coming for prayer and I felt He told me to train people to help me. As I continued to pray He gave me an outline of what to include in the training. But as this was all new to me, I just put it on the shelf.

The regional Pastor at church began to hear so many great testimonies he asked me what I was doing. I shared with him how I was praying for people's root causes and that I was becoming physically overwhelmed. When I mentioned what I thought God had said about training others and that I had an outline, he asked to look through what God had given me.

When he finished reading the outline, he looked up and said 'This is God, Lee.' I was stunned. It was hard for me to imagine anyone coming to me to be trained. I was just a member of the Church not a Pastor or anybody in a leadership position. With that in mind I asked him who on earth would I invite and who would actually respond? He suggested I ask only those who had personally experienced changes in their lives as a result of me praying for them. I was comfortable with that so I sent out invitations expecting maybe a half a dozen people to take up the challenge.

To my amazement forty two people enrolled and one of the men asked if he could video the sessions. Now I was really uneasy. What, me on video? Teaching the things that had messed up my life? But beneath all those feelings there was a little bit of excitement. Perhaps the teaching would save others from soul imprisonment resulting from events in their past. That would be worthwhile!

Chapter 6
BIRTH OF THE MINISTRY

Forty of those who enrolled in the Course graduated after passing an exam and completing the practical sessions. During the training I began to realise God was preparing some of the students to join with Alan and me in ministry. We began to gather a team of prayer ministers and intercessors to meet the demand for ministry to broken, hurting people. I had also had a revelation now that we were in 'ministry'. I often joked that we 'accidently' entered into ministry rather than being called by God. However, God brought me to a place where I realised the birthing of the ministry was entirely His doing and He was in complete control of everything.

After our Graduation Ceremony and asking God for wisdom, Alan and I selected those who were to join the ministry team as Prayer Ministers and those who would begin as Intercessors. As the team was put in place, the number of people seeking ministry escalated rapidly.

Living Springs Ministries: A ministry of healing and restoration, had been birthed and was becoming known both locally and interstate. Seeking God for revelation of the roots in their lives rather than just using a formula ensured that these broken people would receive not only healing but restoration.

God gave us strategies for operating as a team. Each session was held with three team members, two of whom were Prayer Ministers and the other an Intercessor. Prior to each meeting the team members were given the person's Christian name and went to prayer asking God to disclose the root causes of the problems for which he or she were seeking ministry. The three team members then met together before the person arrived to compare what the Lord had revealed to each one. I still remember new team members almost shaking in their boots at that point, wondering if they were hearing accurately or not. It was a learning curve for each of us and it was astounding how accurately we heard God's voice.

When the person came for ministry the Intercessor (a Prayer Minister in training) would make tea or coffee for them beforehand. It allowed them to relax a little before we began. We didn't describe what the Lord had revealed to us, but rather asked relevant questions which revealed that we had heard from God accurately. We believed this was a more sensitive approach for those seeking help than announcing 'God told us this or that'.

Most often we discussed the problems in their lives at first, and then we would explain the necessity of exposing its roots thus ensuring permanent healing rather than a temporary solution. After establishing the fruit and roots to be dealt with, the prayer time began. The two Prayer Ministers shared that responsibility as led by Holy Spirit.

Firstly, we dealt with all the fruit and then the power of each root was broken and pulled up and out of the soul area. During this time the Intercessor was quietly praying in the Spirit. If she received a word from God she raised her hand to let us know and then she was invited to contribute. Occasionally we felt the contribution was not helpful at that time and gently corrected it, but the intercessors understood and accepted that it was part of the learning process in becoming a Prayer Minister.

The results from the ministry were amazing and we gained widespread notability. Some of the testimonies were so incredible that I was summoned to our Senior Pastor's Office. He had heard so many stories about lives being changed and transformed he wanted to hear from us personally about what we were actually doing.

When we shared with him the basic principles of dealing with the roots of people's problems and how we prayed, he expressed some apprehension. He asked whether we believed that Jesus took all of that upon Himself on the Cross when He gave His life for our sin and sicknesses. We told him that of course we believed that, to which he replied 'Then why are you doing what you do?' I had no time to think. My reply just came spontaneously out of my mouth: 'Then why do you give an altar call for Salvation and another for those requiring physical healing?' Shock and surprise covered his face, but before he could answer that I continued: 'Yes, Jesus paid the price for everything on the Cross, but we need to appropriate what He accomplished. That's why you give altar calls in the Church service and we pray for healing and restoration of the soul to manifest.' God had intervened in our conversation and from then on we had the Pastor's full support. He acknowledged the ministry was from God and honoured the fruit of the ministry in those broken lives being healed and restored to wholeness.

From this time we came to realise we needed to be accountable to more than just the Pastors of our local Church. After some research and much prayer we formed an Advisory Council which consisted of Pastors from several denominations as well as our own home Church. Alan and I met with them once a month to make decisions about the ministry together and to be accountable. God honoured our decision. We were richly blessed by their diverse experience contributing to the ministry, and to our own lives. Each one of them functioned in the office of one or more of the Biblical five-fold ministry callings: namely, apostle, prophet, teacher, pastor and evangelist.

At this time, we were still ministering in our home. In the beginning, the ministry involved teams on a roster and we held three or four sessions a week. Within twelve months we had three sessions operating at the same time in three different rooms in our home. There were three sessions in the morning, three in the afternoon and three in the evening, four days a week. When Alan and I took a break from ministry sessions we had to go away from our own home to get some rest.

Parking became a problem because we lived in a small court and there were often ten or more cars parked in the driveway and in the street. I am so grateful we had open and friendly communication with each of the neighbours otherwise we could have been in trouble both with them and the local council. Every Christmas we gave each of the neighbours a substantial gift for allowing us to dominate the parking areas. They were flexible and gracious to us in understanding the need for such a ministry.

As we continued to grow, I needed to train more teams and also train others to train new team members. I could no longer do it all. Some members of the existing teams had grown quickly through their experience as Prayer Ministers and several of them agreed to undertake 'train the trainer' instruction. The initial vision for the ministry had been to bring healing and restoration to broken lives and this was being accomplished by ministering in the Spirit to bring healing to the whole person. Now, an additional part to the vision was about to be birthed. We would train, equip, mobilize and release ordinary lay people, as we were. Prayer Ministry Training was launched.

Prayer Ministry Training is a Christ-centred teaching course led by Holy Spirit. Trainees are encouraged to seek revelation directly from God, especially when ministering to others. The training consists of teaching, group interaction and the opportunity to minister and, if necessary, to receive ministry. This is not theory-only teaching, but a very practical one equipping to function in fruitfulness in personal life, which is empowering for the work of ministry. Briefly outlined, these are the four levels of training.

LEVEL 1 – OPENING PRISON DOORS

Introduction to Prayer Ministry

We are often asked 'What is Prayer Ministry?' It is simply prayer led and empowered by Holy Spirit to bring healing and restoration to hurting, broken lives as well as releasing God's love into their lives. Sometimes the problems people have go much deeper than what they present on the surface. Bad fruit has bad roots and Prayer Ministry gets to the roots of problems. Things which happen in our past wound our soul and healing for the soul has tended to be overlooked in the Body of Christ. Didn't it all happen at the Cross? Yes, it did . . . when Jesus said *'It is finished'* it was, but we need to appropriate it – the same as we do with salvation and physical healing.

In addition to teaching on one-to-one Prayer Ministry we also give opportunity for trainees to receive prayer ministry as part of their preparation to minister to others.

Knowing our Authority

Before we can minister effectively we need to know who we are in Christ and what our authority is in Christ, as well as the benefits of being in Christ. It is imperative that we not only know about this Jesus Who lives in us, but really **know** Him personally and allow Him to live **through** us.

Freedom Through Repentance

Biblical repentance is an inner change of mind, resulting in an outward turning away from sin or turning around to move in a completely new direction. Some people show remorse or anguish for their sin (or consequences of it) but do not change their mind, their course, or their direction. This is not true Biblical repentance.

We need to ask God to show us those areas in our lives where we need to repent, allowing Him to search our hearts to expose any self-righteousness or pride and to convict us in those areas where the Word of God is not our standard. When praying for others we ask God to show them any areas where they may need to repent. Repentance brings such freedom and results in great joy.

Unforgiveness / Bitter Roots

Forgiveness is to excuse others from hurting us and for the offences against us and to release them and set them at liberty. Easier said than done! The enemy's goal is to keep us in captivity and he knows that when we choose to forgive we are released from bondage.

If we don't forgive, faith won't work for us and our prayers are hindered. This causes torment in our life. Our refusal to forgive a person doesn't hurt them at all. Unforgiveness blocks our personal relationship with God – our ability to enjoy His Presence.

There are Four Levels of Wounding that Require Forgiveness:

Bruise: a surface level wounding which can be healed easily if treated promptly and properly.

Cut: a more serious wound, perhaps inflicted intentionally. The hurt produces immediate personal pain and requires special treatment to achieve forgiveness and healing.

Open Wound: a major hurt lodged in the heart that cannot be treated just by desiring to change our feelings. The pain continues despite our consciously wanting to forgive.

Crippling Injury: a deep wound of the spirit resulting in pervasive and general attitudes of unforgiveness The actual wound or its ramifications may not be in our conscious awareness.

Unforgiveness is bondage. It is poison that causes bitterness. It is impossible to be bitter and get better at the same time. We must trust God to change our feelings towards those who have hurt us.

Allow Holy Spirit to show us any unforgiveness in our hearts and acknowledge the wounding we have suffered. Recognize that hurting people hurt people. Choose to forgive those who have hurt us and ask God to help us see that person as He sees them. Determine we will no longer dwell on the hurts of the past. Believe God is healing our soul.

If unforgiveness remains in our hearts it becomes a root of bitterness which is profound grief accompanied by suppressed hostility. It pollutes our whole emotional and physical system, builds walls of isolation and can destroy us.

A bitter root produces bitter fruit such as depression, negativity, low self esteem, anger, self-pity and a controlling attitude. But God can heal all of that once we forgive.

Victory Over Fear

Fear is **F**alse
Evidence
Appearing
Real

Different people fear different things with different levels of intensity, but basically, we all fear what we cannot control. Three common areas of fear are fear of change, fear of the impossible, and fear of man (fear of other's opinions). If you don't think you have a problem with fear, ask yourself 'when was the last time I was worried?' Worry makes us double-minded – it distracts us from the things of God. 'Whatever gets your attention gets you.' The best antidote for worry is **Philippians 4:6,7**

> *'Be anxious for nothing but in everything by prayer and supplication, with thanksgiving, let your requests be known to God; and the peace of God which passes all understanding will guard your heart and mind through Christ Jesus.'*

Fear can be caused through lack of understanding and it keeps us in bondage. To get free from any fear in us we must first ask God to expose it, then renounce it, and choose to trust God. We ask Him to show us the roots of that fear and then allow Him to heal the pain. Cast out the spirit of fear. We can strengthen ourselves in the Lord through His Word which will cause us to become free and fearless. Faith overcomes fear.

Physical Healing

God calls sickness captivity, but every captive of sickness has been granted deliverance **(Job 42:10)**. Jesus calls sickness bondage. Every person bound, He commanded to be loosed and set free **(Luke 13:16)**. Holy Spirit calls sickness oppression, but every oppressed person can now go free **(Acts 10:38)**.

The Word of God shows us that it is God's will to heal. God does not use sickness to chasten us, nor does He allow sickness so we can develop compassion for the sick. Healing is part of the New Covenant which is no longer a book of letters but a Person – Jesus Christ.

There are two avenues of healing under the New Covenant – by personal faith and by the anointing. It is God's prerogative *how* we are healed. The most important fact to know is we received provision for our healing over two thousand years ago – it was achieved on the Cross.

However there can be some hindrances to healing. Jesus is the only Healer, so looking to the man or woman of God instead of Jesus can hinder the receiving of healing. Other hindrances: desiring healing more than the Healer, or having our eyes on the symptoms instead of Jesus.

Once we have received our healing we need to continue to trust in God, stay in prayer and speak and obey God's Word. Also we need to be quick to confess our faults to one another when we sin, observe the natural laws of healthy nutrition and lifestyle, and resist the devil if he tries to put sickness back upon us.

LEVEL 2 - HEALING THE BROKEN HEARTED

Abandonment / Prison of Rejection

Abandonment is the most tormenting pain in the human soul. If our father who seeded life in us abandons us, or the mother who gave birth to us abandons us, it leaves a huge wound on the soul. Whether they physically abandon us or they have no time for us (emotional abandonment) it leaves huge bruises of anxiety in our soul. And, along with the question, 'Why don't you want me?' it deposits anger in our hearts.

Some other roots of abandonment include generational sin, given up for adoption; premature birth or time in a humid crib, or a parent dies at your birth.

There are also numerous types of 'bad fruit'. This is only a representative list. Person feels unwanted or not accepted, insecurity, no self worth, anxiety and depression, frozen emotions, a need to be in control, always looking for revenge, anger, feel unprotected or lost, fear, loneliness, sense of shame, compulsive disorder and self-idolatry.

The root of Rejection is similar to Abandonment. We can be cast aside, thrown away as having no value. That can occur any time in life and through anybody. School Teachers may address children with harsh words that take root in the child's soul. 'Life and death are in the power of the tongue.' Negative words that cause rejection can come from unexpected sources. Along with the root of Rejection grows 'self rejection' (causing fear of failure, hopelessness and despair) and 'fear of rejection' (causing us to become approval seekers) and sometimes results in many forms of rebellion.

After asking God in Prayer Ministry to show where the root of rejection began, we remove the cloak of shame, break the chains of abandonment and pull out the root of rejection. God then heals the damaged emotions and we minister the love and acceptance of Father God by asking Him to fill with his love, His peace and His joy.

There is only one solution after having your wounded soul healed and restored, and that is to receive Father God's love. The knowledge that He loves you is not enough, but rather tangibly *experiencing* that Father's love. When receiving Prayer Ministry you are filled with God's love, peace and joy so that you know His total acceptance of you as a His child.

Orphan Spirit / Receiving the Father's Love

Sometimes we come across somebody who has what we call an Orphan Spirit because they have not experienced love and acceptance from anybody. We know God loves us but we need to experience His love. The love of the Father which was lost in the Garden of Eden needs to be restored to us. It was the reason Jesus went to the Cross. It is not enough to know about God's Love but we need to allow Him to become a Father to us. Love is a relationship. Prayer Ministry provides a way for this to become a reality to us

Hearing God's Voice

John 10:27 says *'My sheep hear My Voice.'*
We must not only hear, but also be able to recognize His voice. It can come as a thought, idea, word, feeling, vision or dream. Unbelief will cause us not to hear, and so will spiritual deafness caused by unforgiveness. Also having an impure heart or not obeying the last thing He said to us can cause us not to hear.

We need to ask God to open the eyes of our heart and breathe new life into our inner sense of seeing and hearing. Ask God to show you His will for all your requests. Our heart is like a radio. We tune in to hear God's Voice and also tune in to see God's vision for us.

The Slumbering Spirit

We all know the difference between a person who is physically awake and one who is asleep. But somebody who is a sleepwalker may give the appearance of being awake yet walk right past people without noticing them. It is not surprising, then, to learn that the human spirit, which is a distinct and separate part from our outer, physical body, can also be awake or asleep. If we do not awaken our spirit we will not be able to function in various areas of our lives.

Here are a few differences between an awakened spirit and a slumbering spirit. During corporate worship an awakened spirit senses the Presence of God while slumbering spirits can only believe He is present. A person with a slumbering spirit can rarely (if at all) receive direct revelation from God; those whose awakened spirits have spiritual dreams, see visions and hear from God in their own spirit. Slumbering spirits find reading the Word of God dry and boring; awakened spirits respond to His love and revelation in His Word.

We can cause our spirit to slumber by not being involved in worship or by being too busy to spend private time with God. Betrayal, abuse and deep wounding of the soul can also cause spiritual slumber. Prayer Ministry facilitates healing and restoration in this area.

Anger and Depression

Anger and Depression are two sides of the same coin. They are behaviours used by hurting people to cope with their damaged lives. Some symptoms are lack of energy, sadness, guilt, self-centeredness, suicide, feeling emotionally dead, withdrawing or overeating, and thoughts of 'I am worthless'.

Prayer Ministry for the restoration and healing of the wounded soul will identify the root cause of the anger or depression, enabling you to deal with it, forgive others, and yourself. It will enable you to take responsibility in asking God to exchange depression, despair, and hopelessness for His confidence, hope and optimism. It will enable you to ask God to take your anger and give you His patience, peace and self-control.

Emotional Healing

I prefer to call this Inner Healing because we are actually dealing with our inner person. The Word of God talks much about the inner man - our inner personality. It is healing for the mind, will and emotions resulting from painful memories of deep hurts and traumatic experiences, often from childhood.

During Prayer Ministry we ask God to reveal anything in the past that is affecting you now, and encourage you to forgive those who hurt you. We ask God to heal the memory completely, bringing restoration to every area which has been affected.

As Holy Spirit reveals the source (root causes) of problems, Jesus heals and sets us free from the consequences of abuses, horrors and traumas in our background. Even Spirit-filled Christians may be in good spiritual condition, yet emotionally crippled. Jesus wants us to be completely whole. He not only died to save us from our sins (spiritual healing) but so that we can have peace (inner healing). He died to free us from pain and disease (physical healing). He died so we could be made **whole.**

Our conscious mind controls our actions, our subconscious mind records things that we can recall, and our unconscious mind records **all** events, some of which we cannot always recall; (e.g. my Satanic Ritual Abuse – repressed memory).

Childhood memories are important. Memory is like an inbuilt tape recorder which starts at conception. Information recorded and processed is important because our subconscious records everything and forgets nothing. Time can heal unrepressed and uninfected memories, but time by itself cannot heal those memories which are so painful that our mind will not tolerate them. We continue to suffer the consequences of the original trauma even when we have blocked out the memory of them.

Thank God for His word in **Psalm 23:3 *'He restores my soul.'*** His answer is healing and restoration for our soul. God's answer is two-fold: the work of the Cross – **Isaiah 5-53:3** and the work of Holy Spirit – **Rom 8:15, John 4:26, Isaiah 61:1.**

LEVEL 3 – BEAUTY FOR ASHES

Spiritual Gifts in Prayer Ministry

Baptism in Holy Spirit is a doorway to the gifts of Holy Spirit. *'**But you shall receive power when Holy Spirit has come upon you ...**'* **Acts 1:8** We are not just to desire to operate in spiritual gifts we must determine in our hearts to walk in the Spirit. We must realise that the nine gifts of the Spirit are supernatural gifts. The key to operating in the gifts is that they operate as Holy Spirit wills, not as we decide. Our part is to make ourselves available to be a vessel through which God's power can flow.

Isaiah 61:1-3 shows us that the purpose of the gifts of Holy Spirit is to:
- preach the Gospel
- heal the sick
- bind up the broken hearted
- set captives free

Holy Spirit Baptism equips us for Prayer Ministry.

Release from Guilt and Shame

Guilt is a position of wrong standing before God – a sense of being out of relationship with God. Guilt is a sense of regret about what we know we have done wrong. It drains our energy, blocks fellowship with God and weakens our spiritual life

Shame is an emotion which, if internalized, becomes part of our nature. Biblically, it is depicted as disgrace, dishonour and nakedness. Shame relates to how we feel about ourselves.

We must choose to let go of all guilt and shame. **Repent,** receive God's forgiveness for any sin, let go of guilt and forgive yourself. **Renounce** any areas of shame over your identity, talents, parenting, looks, relationships etc. i.e. 'I renounce shame off my identity.' Ask God to remove the cloak of shame.

Healing Shock and Trauma

This was covered in an earlier chapter

Grief and Loss of Expectations

There are numerous causes of grief. We may go through a typically normal two year period grieving the loss of a loved one. However, it is **unresolved grief** which causes wounding to the soul. It can surface as anxiety, fear, anger or depression. Physical symptoms may include cancer of bowel, breast, or kidney. Unresolved Grief can even shut down the reproductive organs. It so wounds our spirit that we are unable to experience or express joy.

Thank God that Jesus understands our grief. **Isaiah 53: 3 & 4:** *'He is despised and rejected of men, a man of sorrow and acquainted with grief. Surely He has borne our griefs and carried our sorrows.'*

Psalm 34:18 *'The Lord is close to the broken-hearted and saves those who are crushed in spirit.'*

During Prayer Ministry we recognize the areas of grief as we ask God to reveal them to us. We do not block the feeling but we acknowledge the grief. Forgive those involved and renounce the grief. Here is a sample Prayer:

'Lord, I acknowledge that this grief is present in my life. It is there because............
I have allowed it to influence and control my understanding of life and my actions, but today Lord I am prepared to deal with it. I acknowledge that my unresolved emotions have bound me to grief, but today I choose to forgive .... for their part in wounding me or creating false expectations in me. I ask You to forgive me for allowing grief to influence my life. In Jesus' name I renounce this grief. I will not allow it to oppress me or rule over me, any more. You, Lord, are my Master. I give You and You alone, the right to rule over me. I give this grief to You, Lord Jesus. You bore it on the Cross. By Your stripes I am healed. I open my heart to You, Holy Spirit, to receive Your cleansing, Your release and Your Love. Amen.'

Verbal, Emotional, Physical and Spiritual Abuse

Verbal Abuse is any statement to a victim that results in emotional damage. **Physical Abuse** is inflicting bodily harm while **Emotional Abuse** includes withheld affection or privileges and threatened violence.

Sexual Abuse is any sexual activity carried out in an inappropriate context which may be emotionally or physically harmful or which exploits a person.

Satanic Ritual Abuse is ultimate human degradation, torture, mind control and destructiveness. Spiritual Abuse can occur when a leader uses his or her position to control or dominate someone. It often involves overriding the feelings and opinions of another without regard to that person's state of living, emotions or spiritual well-being.

All abuse leaves scars and there are dozens of symptoms, including: denial, emotional pain, rejection, loneliness, mental conditions, hopelessness, devastation, victim mentality addictions, distorted image of God, locked emotions, low/no self-esteem, perfectionism, unable to trust (even God), unable to enjoy intimacy, fear/terror, anger, rage, unforgiveness and helplessness.

Not every victim is trapped in the same emotional prison so it is essential that the Prayer Ministry team hear from God and only minister healing/restoration in the areas He reveals. Holy Spirit is the Counsellor. It is His anointing 'that heals broken hearts and sets captives free!'

Here is a suggestion (not a formula) to consider:
- break any curses
- cut soul ties
- break off overshadowing of perpetrator's personality
- remove handprints of the perpetrator
- pray to cleanse violated conscience
- pray for restoration of moral boundaries
- break any blood covenants
- repent of any inner vows and renounce them
- inner healing
- pray for Holy Spirit to release imprisoned emotions
- pray for Holy Spirit to bring to surface all memories needing healing. Allow Holy Spirit to show you how Jesus is doing the healing
- deliverance – if necessary
- ANOINTING every step of the way!

Restoring Trust / Intimacy with God

There are countless ways trust can be broken: sibling rivalry, soul wounding, ridicule by family or friends, jealousy, needs not met, trauma, disloyalty, betrayal and any form of abuse, and many others.

Symptoms of broken trust include: not feeling God's Presence, performing to receive love and attention, approval addiction, controlling, dominance of others, not developing as an individual, fear, anxiety and panic attacks.

To restore trust, encourage the person to confess to the Lord that they do not trust. Encourage them to honestly recount their experience of pain and their feelings about the incident. Minister healing to them in the areas of their hurt, pain and trauma. Growth in the area of restoring ability to trust is a process. Ensure they have good support, and encourage them to develop intimacy with the Lord Jesus.

LEVEL 4 - SETTING THE CAPTIVES FREE

Deliverance / Spiritual Warfare

Deliverance is part of the ministry of Jesus - **Acts 10:38: 'Jesus went around healing the sick and casting out demons.'** Being set free from the control or influence of wrong spirits is part of the 'Great Commission'. However we must guard against continually focusing on demons and deliverance. Never forget that in God's scale of values purity is more important than power. Satan is a defeated foe - **1 John 3:8: 'The Son of God was made manifest to destroy the works of the evil one.'** We need to remember that we have been given all authority in His name, and that every knee will bow to the name of Jesus.

Some of the ways we can give place to the devil is through unforgiveness, occult involvement, drug addiction, sin and possessions. Demons can operate outside the body through curses over us, oppression over us, ungodly ties between us and another person, and any otherwise normal activity around our lives. They can also dwell within us if we have opened a door to them. When they are exposed we simply need to take authority over them and command them to leave.

The Word of God tells us that angels, demons and satan are real and that every Christian is in a spiritual battle - Spiritual Warfare. Angels are spirits who do the bidding of God. Demons are satan's servants who try to deceive us in order to destroy us, but Jesus has triumphed over satan who will be judged for his unspeakable evil.

We must first submit to God, then we need to put on our spiritual armour. It is important to see our obligation to take the offensive, to move out and actively attack satan's kingdom. As long as satan keeps the Church on the defensive his kingdom will not be overthrown.

There are many different aspects of prayer, one of which is that it is a weapon of spiritual warfare. Praise also calls forth supernatural intervention. Preaching the Word of God is like a hammer that will break in pieces every rock that opposes the purposes of God. Testimony is speaking our personal experience of victory.

Generational Iniquities

Generational Iniquities are wickedness, sin, perverseness or lack of justice or righteousness that are passed down upon us in our hereditary line – **Exodus 20:5: 'You shall not bow down to them, nor serve them; for I the Lord your God am a jealous God, visiting the iniquities of the fathers upon the children to the third and fourth generation of them that hate me.'**

Praise God, the Word of God says that Jesus not only bore our sins on Calvary but He also took our transgressions and our iniquities – **Isaiah 53:5**. Sin becomes an iniquity when we keep committing the same sin, then it can open us up to a curse which can be passed down through the bloodline. Some of the symptoms can be mental and emotional breakdown, repeated or chronic illnesses (especially hereditary ones), barrenness, marriage breakdowns, continual financial insufficiency, being accident prone or a history of suicides and unnatural or untimely deaths.

God wants to get rid of the trash in our lives. Pray for the leading of Holy Spirit and follow only what He prompts you from the following:

- acknowledge your own sins and the sins of your forefathers
- forgive your forefathers for family iniquities
- repent and ask God to forgive specific sins of your forefathers
- confess our participation in the iniquities of our forefathers
- ask for forgiveness and cleansing
- separate yourself from sin and those things which displease God
- speaking out loud, take authority over the curse in the name of Jesus Christ and command it to be broken now
- command all demon spirits associated with the curse to leave immediately in the name of Jesus
- apply the Blood of Jesus to your life to cleanse you from all sin whether your own or your forefathers
- cooperate with Holy Spirit in changing your life by renewing your mind

Each step is important, but submitting our will to God will maintain our freedom from bondage and permanently put iniquities in the past.

Addiction to Alcohol

Some of the Fruit of Alcoholic Abuse is anger/rage, avoiding responsibility, co-dependency, controlling, deception, deep shame, denial, depression, desolation, devastation, emotionally asleep, fear of intimacy, fear, mistrust, paranoia, gambling, grief, murder or incest/rape committed during violent outbursts of anger, isolation, manipulation, religious addiction, self-hatred/disgust/self-abuse, victim mentality and insanity and suicide. What a list (and I'm sure there are more), all of which are wounding to the soul.

The roots of Alcohol Abuse could be: generational curse of alcoholism, rebellion, cultural tie, ungodly soul tie, idolatry, illegitimacy, fatherlessness, abandonment, shock/trauma or a root of bitterness.

Ask God to reveal anything relevant to you or the members of your family line. Use the following steps as a guideline only and follow Holy Spirit's leading to minister healing and freedom:

- ☐ Repent and renounce all relevant fruit
- ☐ take accountability for any behavioural patterns
- ☐ make any choices that might be necessary
- ☐ put the axe to any roots the Lord exposes
- ☐ break any curses as necessary
- ☐ make appropriate declarations over your own life and the lives of your family
- ☐ ask God to totally heal the disease of your soul
- ☐ claim the promise that God restores your soul **Psalm 23:3**
- ☐ claim the promises of **Jeremiah 1:18, 19: *'I have made you this day a fortified city with brazen walls. And they shall fight against you, but they will not prevail, for I am with you, says the Lord, to deliver you.'***
- ☐ thank Him for setting you and your family free

Restoration of the Sexually Abused

Sexual abuse leaves emotional scars. God's heartbeat is for both the abused, and the abuser, to be healed, delivered and restored. This is why Jesus was anointed and this is why we are anointed – **Isaiah 61:1-3**

Sexual abuse can be verbal (inappropriate sexual talking which makes the victim feel dirty), it can be visual (made to view nakedness, pornographic material, masturbation or intercourse), or it can be physical (inappropriate touching, invasive bathing, penetration or rape). Incest is more common than we realise, even in Christian circles. It is any form of sexual abuse taking place within the family structure by anyone perceived by the family to be part of the family.

Devalued self-esteem is the currency of sexual abuse. It is a tragedy. The violation impacts every aspect of the victim's life and causes them to live in desolation (ruin, solitary misery, wretchedness, numbness – cannot receive spiritually) and devastation (to lay waste, ravaged, destroyed)

We must recognize that **healing is a process** and that Jesus Christ is the **only** Healer. Secular methods may diagnose the problem but **only Jesus can heal and restore** the abused. **He alone turns victims into victors.** Victims of abuse suffer mental and emotional 'death'. Healing and restoration means that for perhaps the first time in their lives they are fully alive. God not only restores His children to life but also restores their childhood which has often been stolen.

My suggested steps (led by Holy Spirit) in the Healing Process for the Sexually Abused:

- acknowledge that you have been sexually abused and identify the effects the abuse is having in your life
- make a decision to allow God to heal you

- [ ] understand the abuse was not your fault
- [ ] acknowledge God as the source and power of restoration
- [ ] believe the abuse happened
- [ ] begin to deal with the memories and suppressed emotions /feelings
- [ ] break the silence
- [ ] recount each experience
- [ ] pray daily in your own prayer time for Restoration
- [ ] make contact with the child within and release the anger. Getting in touch with the child within can help us feel compassion for ourselves and allow us to be angry with the abuser
- [ ] trust God, trust yourself and trust others. Study the love of God and choose to trust Him. Choose to begin to trust others
- [ ] grieving and mourning – allow yourself to grieve and release the pent-up anger at the lack of support and love that should have been there for you.
- [ ] work through denial, depression, fear, loneliness, guilt and shame – learn to express your emotions and feelings
- [ ] fix your worth, value and esteem in the Word of God
- [ ] forgive the abuser – this can be quite a process!
- [ ] allow God to cause your pain to be forgotten – one day at a time
- [ ] accept the fact that healing and restoration take time
- [ ] rely upon God to complete the healing process

When healing is complete three levels of relationships will be restored:

- **relationship with God**
  - be back in touch with God
  - right perspective of God – God of love
  - be able to trust God
  - faith in God will be restored
  - able to receive God's love
  - able to feel His Presence
- **relationship with self**
  - be able to manage our emotions
  - have a healthy self-esteem
- **relationships with others**
  - be able to trust other people
  - enjoy intimate relationships
  - give and receive love

It is worth taking time to be healed and restored. Keep your eyes on Jesus – He is the One Who heals and restores.

Life After Ritual Abuse

This topic was added to the Prayer Ministry Training later. It is dealt with at length in Chapter 7.

Maintaining Your Freedom
Stand Daily on the Word
Develop an Effective Prayer Life
Re-program your Subconscious Mind
Remember the Faith Pictures Jesus Gave You
Make Jesus Lord of Your Life
Keep Your Eyes On Jesus
Walk in Forgiveness
Bring Every Thought Into Captivity

Develop a Lifestyle of Continual Prayer and Praise
Resist the Enemy
Maintain Fellowship
Confess Victory With Your Mouth

One of the most important things we continually emphasize throughout this Training Course is that the teaching is not a formula. It is absolutely essential that each person receiving Prayer Ministry is treated as a unique individual created and valued by God. They came to the place of needing ministry differently from everybody else. They were hurt, wounded, rejected etc in a manner that nobody else has been. Therefore it is essential that we seek God for the keys to their healing and restoration, and minister only as we are led by Holy Spirit. I cannot emphasize this enough.

—oOo—

There is one couple a Pastor sent to us from the other side of town who I will never forget. They had been married only three years and been receiving ministry for the last two years. The lady was unable to participate in marital sex with her husband and it was causing major issues.

When they arrived for Prayer Ministry she was so upset and rude. We had prayed beforehand and God had revealed keys to us, but when I spoke to her she shouted at me, 'I'm not telling you anything. I'm sick of my husband making me seek help.' I was a little frustrated because I knew God wanted to heal and restore her. She continued bad mouthing until I got angry and threw the list at her of what God had revealed to us. The other two team members were horrified because I had always emphasized that was not permitted under any circumstances. However, she picked up the list and her face changed. She began to weep. 'Nobody knows this, not even my husband. This has to be God' she said. Incest was at the top of that list.

We ministered to her as led by Holy Spirit and she was totally healed and restored from the trauma and wounding of soul that was a result of incest at a very young age. She apologized to her husband, asking his forgiveness (and ours for her behaviour.) They departed hand in hand and radiating joy.

Fifteen months later we received a lovely letter of thanks and a photo of their beautiful new baby. Such touching memories inspire us to keep working with Holy Spirit regardless of how difficult some situations are. A couple of years later we received another letter and photo, and then another eighteen months later. God had certainly healed and restored this couple and the beautiful fruit was three lovely children.

The importance of following Holy Spirit directions is illustrated in the following testimony - one of my favourites. One Sunday, Alan and I were called out to minister to a man who had cancer of the stomach. He was to be admitted to hospital the following morning and was due for surgery at midday. He was not a Christian so we led him in giving his life to the Lord Jesus Christ. I was about to lay my hands on him to pray for healing of the cancer when Holy Spirit said to me 'Cancer is not the problem, Lee, unresolved grief is'. I wondered what I was going to do with that revelation knowing the man had been a Christian for about five minutes!

I waited a moment and then asked him (as casually as I could) if he had anything in his life which he had never dealt with, such as unforgiveness towards anybody, anger, bitterness or perhaps some grief that had never been resolved. The gentleman began weeping. Weeping became uncontrolled sobbing which continued for twenty minutes. I knew in my heart that his grief had gone but I prayed for his healing anyway and we left for home.

The next afternoon I received a phone call. The voice on the other end of the line was so high pitched it was difficult to understand what was being said. 'Who are you?' I asked. I am the man you prayed for yesterday,' he replied. 'Oh,' I said, 'How did the operation go?' His voice went up another notch. 'That's why I am ringing you. The Surgeon has just been in to tell me that when they opened me up to remove the cancer, it wasn't there!' Now it was my turn to be ecstatic! Our God is amazing! All praise, glory and honour to Him!

These two testimonies make us so aware of how wonderful our God is and how much He desires to bring healing and restoration to sick, hurting people. The importance of being led by Holy Spirit is the most important key there is.

Chapter 7
A BLAST FROM THE PAST

The ministry continued to grow and wonderful testimonies flowed in. More and more broken people came to us for help as their pastors and Church leaders referred them to us. The results that were being achieved were simply the fruit of partnering with Holy Spirit to uncover the roots in people's lives and allowing Him to direct the Prayer Ministry that brought freedom, healing and restoration.

In 1994 a well-known Pastor 'phoned to ask if I would minister to a child whose mother attended his Church. This woman had separated from her husband when she discovered that he had joined some occult group and had allowed their daughter to take part in a dedication ceremony. Two team members joined me in seeking God for fruits and roots in this case. As the appointment with her drew near I began to feel ill and uneasy. I purchased a soft Teddy Bear for the child, but as I took it to the checkout I realised I was holding it tightly to my own chest as though for comfort.

When mother and daughter arrived for their appointment I presented the child with the Teddy Bear. She received it but displayed no pleasure of any kind. The mother told us her child had gone into meltdown after being exposed to the occultic rituals and since then had hardly spoken. She spent every day in bed, not eating or drinking, and refusing to go to school. When the woman confronted her husband she learned the details of what had been performed on their child and immediately left the home with her daughter.

We explained to the mother how we functioned and that God had given us some keys to seeing her daughter healed and restored. We also explained that it could take several appointments due to the seriousness of the condition. Then we began to minister. At first, communication with the child was difficult, but we gently persisted and she began to speak. She cuddled the teddy and looked at it rather than at me, as she answered me. We soon recognized the depth of trauma she had been through.

This was the worst case of child abuse I had ever heard of. However, even that did not explain what was going on inside of me as we ministered. I felt nauseous and disoriented and I could not understand why. My colleagues were just as shocked by what the child had disclosed, but they weren't affected like me.

That night, I had great difficulty getting to sleep. Eventually, exhausted, I fell asleep, only to wake some time later screaming and thrashing, and totally out of control. My husband put the light on, wrapped his arms around me, and spoke tender words of love and peace until I calmed down. I told him about the nightmare I had just had. I was travelling in a car with a male relative and I was screaming and crying and I had my head on his lap. He was stroking my head saying 'It's alright, Lee, settle down; it was only a bad dream.' I had absolutely no idea what the dramatic nightmare was about.

The next morning I still did not feel back to normal, but I could not put into words what I was feeling. There was no peace and no joy, just an unexplainable heaviness over me. It was almost like a depression and my family and team around me were noticing it too. None of us had an explanation. Finally I rang Ps Harold Dewberry in America who I had met previously. He didn't address the problem but informed me that he and his brother Ps Roy Dewberry would be coming to Australia in about six weeks to conduct Seminars on Satanic Ritual Abuse both in Melbourne and in Adelaide. He said it would be really good if Alan and I, and as many of our team as possible, would attend. We discussed it at our next Team Meeting and most of them agreed to do that. I was comforted to know that

Harold and Roy were coming. Deep inside I knew this was going to be helpful, both to me and to our whole team. I could not have imagined just how important it became.

Alan and I took Harold and Roy out for dinner the evening before the Seminar in Adelaide. I shared with them about the girl who had been dedicated to satan and they understood because they had been dealing with the same issues in America. Then I told them about the nightmare I had and that my life had been changed by the heaviness I was experiencing. They listened carefully and said I would benefit from the Seminars and they would minister to me privately.

A number of our Prayer Ministry Team attended the Seminar with the Dewberry brothers. We were keen to understand Satanic Ritual Abuse, its effects, and the way to minister freedom and restoration to the victims. We were unaware of how often children were dedicated to satan in these horrific rituals. As I sat listening to the teaching in one of the final sessions, I suddenly manifested like a wild animal for no apparent reason. I was so violent Harold asked that I be removed from the meeting. Several of my team had to drag me into a private room where they tried to calm me down. Nothing they knew to do had any effect and I continued with my outrageous screaming. Then one of the older Prayer Ministers, Stella, asked Muriel, 'What did Harold say just before Lee started to manifest?' Muriel checked her notes. 'That,' said Stella, 'is what we have to do, right now!' They followed the instruction to break the soul tie between satan and me and I stopped screaming. All of us now had more questions than answers!

After the Seminar, Harold and Roy shared with me that God had shown them I had been a victim of Satanic Ritual Abuse. I went home in shock and utter disbelief. The following day Harold telephoned me from Melbourne and suggested I fly to Melbourne so that he and Roy could minister to me. Disappointed, I told them

I could not afford the air fares at that time. Several hours later they called back to tell me God had instructed them to pay my fares. Alan and I discussed it and I was on my way within 48 hours. When I collected my ticket at the check-in desk I saw it was only a one-way ticket. I was to learn this was very much a God strategy.

During the flight I had nausea, terror and torment of mind such as I had never experienced on previous flights. Demonic voices began in my head and I was having horrific visions. I don't mind admitting I was terrified. All I wanted to do was go home to Alan. In retrospect, I understood why the Dewberry brothers had purchased a one-way air ticket! When Harold and Roy met me at the airport I was not in a good place. I had been terrorized by the demonic visions and encounters. They reassured me that everything would be alright once they had spent some time ministering to me.

The next morning after a beautiful encounter with Jesus and experiencing His love, which was just so healing in itself, Harold and Roy began to minister to me. A vision unfolded which was of me walking down the aisle of a church, dressed as a bride, with a known relative. I appeared to be about six or seven years old. As we neared the front of the church I was handed over to this other person who was dressed up as satan and the ceremony began. It was a replica of a marriage ceremony, including the vows. Afterwards I was taken into another room by the satanic figure where he had sexual intercourse with me. As the vision unfolded it was as though it was happening right then and I could feel the terror and the physical pain.

Harold and Roy broke off the words of the covenant between me and satan and broke the satanic curse. They commanded satan to release my spirit, body and soul and broke his overshadowing over my life. Every ungodly handprint left on my life was removed by God and cleansed with the Blood of Jesus. Harold cancelled the rights of the ungodly high priest and broke his contract over me by the Name and Blood of Jesus and asked God to restore the joy of my salvation. As shock, trauma and horror were broken off my mind and emotions, they called down the fire of God to burn up the blackness left over my life from this evil. From that moment God began to heal my emotions and my memories and take me deeper into His love.

In subsequent sessions, other visual flashbacks occurred which were extremely difficult to walk through, but God was so gracious, setting me free from all that came to the surface. It was so horrendous, all I wanted to do was to die and go to Jesus in Heaven. When there was a break from the focus on satanic flashbacks, I spent time in the Presence of the Lord Jesus, allowing Him to minister His love, peace and joy. During these times I was greatly refreshed and very much aware of His unconditional love and His Presence.

Harold and Roy decided I had been through enough for the time being and suggested my team could continue to minister to me as further visions were triggered and memories surfaced.

It took fourteen months for me to be completely healed and free. We were not working on it all the time of course, only as a memory surfaced. Some of the triggers took us by surprise. We found we could not drive behind a Toyota car during this time. I would see the Toyota emblem as a bull's head, which was significant in some of the occultic flashbacks. I am not saying that is what the Toyota symbol stands for, but it was just that it happened to trigger a memory. Another time, Alan and I were in a restaurant enjoying a meal when a young man came in. The bull's head on the back of his jacket caused me to manifest outrageously and we had to leave the restaurant without finishing our meal.

Another time I was simply walking down the passage of our home when I had a vision of myself being attacked with sharp instruments as part of an occultic ritual. I fell, screaming and writhing, to the floor. Alan said he would never forget those screams: they were not those of an adult, but those of a terrified child. He picked me up and called a couple from the Prayer Ministry Team. They ministered to me and broke all the satanic powers associated with that particular memory.

One day God challenged me to forgive those who had committed these gross rituals on me. Forgiving people with a simple 'Father, I forgive them' was not enough. When I prayed this prayer I knew I did not mean a word of it. In my heart I wanted to kill the ones who had sold me to satan. I had to ask Holy Spirit to help me. I began to pray 'Father, I choose to forgive these satanists and I ask You, Holy Spirit, to help me make that a reality, not just words'. I prayed this prayer every day for six weeks. Finally, something broke inside of me and I knew that it was a reality and it was done! Praise the Lord! It is so important that we don't just follow the 'laws' of religion, but that we walk in the reality of relationship with the Lord Jesus Christ.

> **Religion Conforms** us by following a set of rules.
> **Relationship Transforms** us into the likeness of Jesus.

But even after I had truly forgiven I found myself asking the Lord why my pain continued and why I was not yet completely healed. Long months of not knowing when another issue would arise to cause me public embarrassment had caused me to be disheartened. I had begun to lose trust in Him for completed healing and freedom. One day He said:

> *'If you return fully to me and give up this distrust and despair then I will give you again a settled place of quiet and safety and you will be My minister. If you separate the precious from the vile, cleansing your own heart from unworthy and unwarranted suspicions concerning My faithfulness, you shall be My mouthpiece.'*

I realised the truth of that word. I *had* given up hope of being healed and free. I repented of my mistrust and again chose to trust God in every situation.

Eventually, the flashbacks became less frequent and I began to think everything had been dealt with. Because of the great change in my life Harold and Roy Dewberry began to include me on their team as they ministered in seminars around Australia. I was privileged to use my own experiences to minister healing and freedom to others. I was always so blessed when I saw lives restored.

At one of those meetings where I was on Harold and Roy's Prayer Ministry Team, I stood beside a lady who had gone forward for prayer. Roy prayed for her and commanded release from some wicked satanic being. With no prior warning it was me who flew backwards through the air and landed with my head under a table! But that was the finish. I knew that I was finally, and totally, free.

When I arrived back in Adelaide to share the experience with Alan and our Prayer Ministry Team, I received the following word from the Lord:

> *'My child, I love you – you are very special to me. You have gone through much, My dear one, but believe Me it has not been in vain. Though you find it difficult to understand at this time let Me assure you there is a purpose in all of it.*
>
> *Many have been tortured by evil men, broken, bruised, some beyond hope of repair. Like you, they have reached out for help in the natural realm and found none. For these experiences have not been natural experiences, but supernatural ones. Therefore there is no effective and lasting help in the natural, but only from Me in the supernatural. There are two powers in the supernatural realm – the power of evil (satan's power) and the power of good (My power).*

You have been damaged by satan's power in an effort to destroy you, but My power has brought restoration - it has made you whole. Your devastation was carefully planned by the evil one. He tried to destroy the whole you - spirit, soul and body. He failed. I thwarted his evil plan. I came to bring restoration to every part of you. Just as satan carefully planned your destruction, I too have carefully planned your healing and restoration to wholeness.

I have healed your wounded, broken spirit and set you free from the bondages of satan. I have taken back your will from satan and returned it to you. You will no longer have difficulty with your decision-making. I have restored your mind and your damaged emotions. Now I desire to heal your body to complete your wholeness. Will you now submit your body to My care as you have submitted your spirit and soul? Allow me to teach you how to have dominion over your body so that you can rule and reign over every area of your life and walk in total victory.

I love you and this is My desire for you. It is My desire that you not only enjoy the release, freedom and victory, but that you may lead others to walk this path with Me.'

A few days after that word from the Lord I was at a soaker service at Paradise AOG Church. The power of the Lord came upon me so heavily that I was prostrate on the floor. I shed many tears and then came a measure of peace I had never experienced before.

Suddenly I saw Jesus Christ coming toward me. The light and the sense of His love were overwhelming. He bent down to me and kissed my face. Then He washed me all over and kissed my body. His love was tangible. *'I see you, My child, as totally healed, free and clean'.* The impact of that word 'clean' has never left me. I had always felt dirty because of all the rituals, but now Jesus was telling me I was clean! It was another life changing experience.

Now, the final topic of our Prayer Ministry Training Course.

LEVEL 4 - SETTING THE CAPTIVES FREE

Life After Ritual Abuse

Ritual Abuse represents the ultimate in human degradation. It includes torture, mind control and destruction. It is a brutal violation of children, adolescents and adults, consisting of physical, sexual, emotional and spiritual abuse which is accompanied by satanic rituals and worship. Ritual Abuse rarely consists of a single episode, but is repeated over an extended period of time.

The physical abuse is severe, sometimes including torture and killing. The sexual abuse is extremely painful, sadistic and humiliating, intended as a means to gain control over the victim.

The emotional abuse involves the use of ritual indoctrination which includes mind control techniques and mind altering drugs. The spiritual abuse consists of forcing victims to participate in rituals, activities and instructions that induce the belief they are completely separated from God and totally controlled by satan. Victims are often told they have demons that control them.

Both during and after the abuse, most victims enter into a state of terror, mind control and dissociation in which disclosure is extremely difficult. The effects of ritual abuse are horrific because of the use of bizarre practices. Mind control is used in ritual abuse to impart cognitive beliefs such as:

- there is no escape
- the cult is my only true family and it completely controls me

- I am incapable of protecting myself
- memories are dangerous
- disclosure is dangerous

Satanic Religious beliefs are also imparted:
- satan is stronger than God
- God does not love me
- God wants to punish me
- my life is controlled by satan
- my life is dedicated to satan

Such beliefs are lies from the pit of hell! The name of Jesus, the Word of God and the Blood of Jesus Christ are greater than satan and his lies. When Jesus said from the Cross, 'It is finished', satan was totally defeated. Therefore:
- in Jesus name we can pull down every stronghold satan has built in minds
- the Blood of Jesus is far more powerful than any other blood covenant satan has tried to make with us
- the Word of God overrules the effects of any mind control

Ministering Restoration to the Ritually Abused

This ministry is the only one I would classify as a specialist area. It should be conducted only by a trained Prayer Minister / Ministry. Ritual abuse is complicated and the victims are fragile. They must be handled with love, care and the utmost respect so that they are not re-traumatized or damaged any further. I say again, please do not practise the following strategies if you are *not* a trained Prayer Minister.

Ask Holy Spirit to reveal any hidden tragedy, abuse or trauma. Once the memory has surfaced walk through it with the person,

praying every step of the way. Listen to God's directions – follow them!

- [ ] bind the strongman of anti-Christ
- [ ] shut Jezebel's mouth and command her not to speak
- [ ] cut off the master spirit of mind control – release all associated demons who have been assigned against this person
- [ ] have the person you are ministering to confess any involvement in occult/witchcraft, ask God for forgiveness and renounce their involvement
- [ ] have them acknowledge that they have been deceived by the lies of satan
- [ ] break deception off their lives – specifically break the deception of a false Jesus off their lives
- [ ] ask God to reveal the real, and only, true Jesus to them
- [ ] acknowledge that Jesus is the Truth
- [ ] ask God to show them the truth about who they are in Christ
- [ ] acknowledge the Lordship of Jesus Christ in their lives – submit to His authority
- [ ] ask them to choose to forgive those who abused them
- [ ] cut every soul tie
- [ ] cut a soul tie with satan
- [ ] repent of any vow/dedication made to/with the enemy
- [ ] renounce all satanic vows and dedications
- [ ] break every ungodly blood covenant
- [ ] break the blood covenant with satan
- [ ] cut off every familiar spirit and release it from its assignment against them and their family
- [ ] repent of inviting a spirit guide to guide them
- [ ] have them ask Holy Spirit to be their Guide
- [ ] release every occultic spirit guide from its assignment

- break every bondage to satan
- teach them how to renew their mind with God's Word

—oOo—

It was very soon after my experience in Heaven that my daughter, Cheryl, came to me with the news that her dad had let it slip that we had given a child up for adoption. Cheryl desired to trace him and make contact. I was mortified. When I gave the baby up I prayed God would cause him to be brought up in a Godly home. I decided in my heart it would be unfair to ever attempt to find him. I wanted his adopted mum and dad to parent him as their very own, without any interaction from me. I told Cheryl that I did not want to go against that decision, but she persisted. Finally, I gave her permission to make enquiries, but I didn't want to be involved. Cheryl, along with her husband and children, traced Andrew extremely quickly and flew to Queensland to meet with him. When they returned they encouraged me to meet him.

Andrew and I began with phone calls, followed by talking on Skype. It was a shock to see how much he resembled my brother. Eventually I flew to Queensland to spend time with him, and his wife and son. There were many similarities in our lives. The most significant one for me was Andrew's passion for the ocean. He even took people on underwater tours. It was a very special time together, not at all what I envisioned when a meeting was first suggested. It was such a blessing to discover his parents were devoted Christians and that he had been brought up in a Christian home. God is so faithful.

Chapter 8
THE BIRTH OF CHRISTIAN COUNSELLING COLLEGE

The demand for ministry continued to escalate and we were very busy. Even with nearly forty trained Prayer Ministers on our team it was becoming increasingly difficult to keep up with the demand. Our home, too, was proving too small to cater for all the sessions and was no longer a place of privacy and rest.

Alan and I began discussing the possibility of renting premises. We looked at many buildings, but the costs were beyond us due to us not requiring payment for the ministry we conducted. There was no charge, either, for the Prayer Ministry Training Courses apart from the purchase of the Student Manual. Prayer Ministry sessions were free to all who came seeking healing and restoration. Everything Alan and I did was voluntary and every one of our Prayer Ministers were volunteers. However, we were convinced that God was totally in control and if we were to shift the ministry to another location, He would provide. And He did.

A local Pastor heard about our need for premises and contacted us. We shared with him how the Lord had begun our ministry as a result of my changed life and that it had grown beyond anything we could have imagined. I also shared how I had recently completed my own fourteen month journey of recovery from Satanic Ritual Abuse and still felt a little fragile. He assured us that he would love me through the transition to total restoration.

The Pastor offered us the currently unused second story of his Church building. It was a gift from God. It so suited our needs and was given to the ministry free of charge. All we had to do was freshen it up with some paint, install new curtains, furnish the

Prayer Ministry rooms, and update the kitchen area. The main area was a suitably large space in which to teach our Prayer Ministry Training Courses and hold Seminars.

The Pastor did not require any of us to leave the Churches we were attending to join his, which we appreciated. However after several months Alan and I felt God instruct us to make it our home Church. In time, many team members did the same, as God led them.

Soon many members of the congregation were making appointments for ministry and becoming transformed. So our reputation continued to travel not only around the state but around the country and even overseas to Indonesia. It was quite overwhelming at times because Alan and I knew we were just ordinary people, albeit ones who God had called and equipped.

God began to challenge me to establish a Christian Counselling College. Despite asking Him 'Who am I to be doing this?' I explored the requirements for registration, not really expecting a positive outcome. However, it was to be another 'but God' situation and a year later Christian Counselling College was birthed. What a wonderful reminder of the truth of God's Word: *'what the enemy meant for evil God turned around for good.'* (Genesis 50:20)

During the first year of Christian Counselling College I was so thankful for my many years experience as a Year 12 school teacher. Attendance was greater than expected and there were many challenges. There was a higher expectation of the College as it was a certificated Course, which included examinations after each of the four levels. Our students went to the local TAFE College premises to sit their examinations because we wanted our examination process to fulfil the formal expectation for Certificated Courses.

Students who completed and passed all four levels were then required to attend the Practical Training. This of course was 'hands on' practice of what was taught in the Course. It was an essential component because on completion the students were fully equipped to function as Prayer Ministers. With students coming from many different Churches all over the state, it went a long way to fulfilling my heart's desire that many would minister to hurting broken people in the way God had taught me. Many graduate students went on to establish Prayer Ministries in their own local Churches.

At the end of each year we held a Graduation Ceremony in the Church that housed the college. The first year's Ceremony will always remain in my memory, not least because of the crowd of family and friends celebrating with them. I joined the graduates on stage and I was so proud and privileged to present their Certificates. During that special evening I looked over at my mother who had asked if she could attend. I could see just how proud of me she was. This was really special to me because I had caused her much grief before God healed and restored me.

Subsequent to this event, she asked me again what had happened in my life when I was a teenager. As my mother, she knew something shocking had occurred because her lovely daughter had changed into somebody totally different and it had broken her heart. At last I was able to tell her about the rapist threatening to hurt not only me, but her too, if I told anybody what he had done. When I told her that I loved her too much to put her life at risk, she hugged me as if she would never let go, and wept. At last she understood.

Once she had calmed down I was able to share with her how God had turned my life around and freed me from bondages that had imprisoned me. Seeing me on the platform at the Graduation she understood just how miraculous was that freedom. For the first time she told me how, after my birth, the nurse put me into her arms and pronounced, 'This is a special child. God has His hand upon her life.' She had never understood that statement and certainly questioned it during the long years of my broken and wayward life.

Chapter 9
TRANSFORMED BY THE POWER OF HOLY SPIRIT

During the 1990s, revival broke out in and around Adelaide and impacted many churches, including the one we attended. The power of Holy Spirit manifested in many different ways and was a new experience for many of us. People were healed of many diseases and terminal illnesses. One girl was healed of Multiple Sclerosis after spending hours on the floor under Holy Spirit's power. When people heard about what God was doing they came to observe and many dedicated their lives to Jesus Christ. Many others had heavenly visions as the power of God touched their lives and some saw Jesus, Himself, during that time.

Revival spread like wildfire into churches large and small and Alan, myself and our team were called to many of them to minister at the altar calls. We had to work in rostered rotation as the Spirit of God manifested Himself all through the suburbs. It was tiring but we were so blessed to be part of such a wonderful move of God. It continued for many months with hundreds of people giving their lives to the Lord, being healed of physical diseases and being delivered from bondages.

One evening in January of 1996 I was prostrate on the floor as Holy Spirit came upon me in a powerful and tangible way. I heard the guest speaker referring to me and saying, 'You will be like this for many days'. I did not understand what he meant by that, but when the meeting was over, some of my team tried to help me up off of the floor and they, too, fell down under the power of the Spirit. Another person tried to take me to my car, but he fell under the power too. It didn't matter who tried to help me, they all ended up on the ground, under the power of God! Finally the Pastor came to me, saying, 'Everyone who tries to get you up falls down. Perhaps you could stay in one of your Prayer Ministry rooms until it lifts.' Muriel, one of my senior Prayer Ministers, finally got me upstairs (more on our hands and knees than anything!) and stayed the night with me. During the night I experienced an open heaven on three occasions, and during one of them I was taken up into heavenly realms..

In my **first heavenly experience** I seemed to be lifted up out of my body into the most glorious light. The light was warm and inviting with an ability to draw me into itself. As the heavens opened I saw the most beautiful clouds with brilliant light shining through them. I sensed that light and life and love were connected. It was as though the very heart of God lay open for everyone in heaven to bask in its glory. As we bathed in His presence we were restored, renewed and refreshed. I had my first glimpse of the throne of God. The brightness all around was radiating through what looked like clouds suffused with fire that turned them the colour of amber.

Oh, the awesome throne in heaven! Seated on the throne, Jesus' appearance was as though millions of jewels were gathered in one place with the brightest sunlight shining through them. This place was entirely and utterly holy, being filled with purity. It was filled with His glory, His beauty, His splendour, His majesty, His radiance and His holiness. I felt love flowing over me like warm, soft honey. I saw a beautiful rainbow around the throne as though through a cloud on a rainy day. It was the glory of God.

Above the throne of God I saw two angelic beings – seraphim. They had six wings; two at the shoulders and four below the waist. Each seraphim covered his face with two wings, two covered his feet and with two he hovered in flight, as if to guard the throne of God. But they also seemed to be leading worship: *'Holy, holy, holy – is the Lord of hosts; the whole earth is filled with His glory'.* There were lamps of burning fire before the throne – the seven Spirits of God – and thunder, lightning and voices came from the throne.

A number of steps lead up to the throne, but they were partially concealed by the brilliant glory clouds. These clouds teemed with life. Twenty four elders, clothed in white robes, worshipped the One on the throne and cast their crowns of gold before Him.

There were thousands of angels of different degrees of brightness – the reflection of the glory of God – and varying degrees of rank and authority. Along with the Seraphim, who appeared to be the head of the angelic beings, there were Cherubim with two outstretched wings. There were many other angels, some with wings and some without. I heard the sound of their wings and felt them brush against me.

I saw the four living creatures with wings and many eyes, continually crying loudly, '*Holy, holy, holy, Lord God Almighty, who was and is – and is to come.*' I knew these creatures brought revelation and wisdom. In this throne room I could do no more than fall to my knees, weeping, overwhelmed by God's love, grace and mercy. His Presence was awesome.

I experienced things in a tangible way:
- holiness of God – felt it, saw it
- intensity of God's love for me
- goodness of God
- kindness of God
- faithfulness of God
- gentleness of God
- joy of being in His Presence
- absolute peace

I saw:
- majesty, beauty – splendour of His Presence
- brilliance of His glory – '*You're the Glory and the Lifter of my head*'

I heard:
- ☐ sounds of wind
- ☐ sounds of waterfalls

There was an incredible sense of celebration in heaven and I had a weightlessness, so that I felt I could fly. I was so aware of God as the Source of all life and all light in heaven.

This experience changed the way I thought about the throne room of God. Now I understood that the throne room of God is His house. It is where He lives. God's throne is His house. We know all of heaven is His, but the throne is where He lives. Now I realised that the entire Godhead, God the Father, the Lord Jesus Christ and Holy Spirit dwell in the Throne Room

During the **second Heavenly experience** I was not simply an observer, but actively engaged in worship before the Throne of God. I do not know how much time elapsed before the heavens opened, but this time it was a little different. There is so much activity there all the time - each time I looked it was different.

This time, the twenty four elders were seated on twenty four thrones and I saw myself standing on what looked like the sea, yet at the same time it was solid, like glass. I was standing in front of the Throne of God, gazing upon His Presence. Oh, the glory - the King of Glory.

I was surrounded by thousands and thousands of others from every tribe and every nation. We were worshipping the Glorious One who sits upon the throne and the worship was glorious - I have no words to describe it. Somehow, the music in heaven seemed to be absolutely everywhere. It was like the thunders of great waterfalls - all the languages from every nation were worshipping in unity:

Holy, holy, holy – Lord God Almighty
You are Holy – You are worthy
No one compares with You
Jesus Christ – the Hope of Glory
You're the glory and the lifter of my head
You are beautiful beyond description
You're much more precious than gold
Lord, You are more beautiful than diamonds
Holy, holy, holy – Lord God Almighty
Holy, holy, holy – Holy, holy, holy

Worship was the heart and focus of the music, and everywhere the joy of it could be felt. My heart resonated with it and I wanted it to never stop. I felt as though it was inviting me to dance. At times the manifestations of God's glory was so powerful I felt like I was on fire.

During my **third Heavenly experience** I was dancing on streets of gold. On this occasion I was caught up by the Spirit and taken through an open door into Heaven. It was a different part of Heaven but still filled with the radiance of the Glory of the Lord. As I walked through the open door it was like entering a place of celebration. People were singing and dancing and there was so much joy. As I watched the celebrations I saw Jesus, the glorified Lord.

- His glory – like a radiant light
- clothed with a dazzling white robe – down to His feet
- a band of gold around His breast
- His head and hair were white like wool
- His eyes were like flames of fire
- His feet were like fine, shiny brass

Almost the instant I saw Him, He came towards me. I fell at His feet to adore Him. Ever so gently He bent down and lifted me up and placed His hand under my chin causing me to look up. His face was so beautiful, so radiant, so holy, and so full of love.

Then I saw His nail pierced hands that had flowed with blood – those hands that flow with love for me. I saw His passion and I knew His forgiveness. I felt His tears that had flowed for me.

Then He spoke and called me by name. His voice sounded strong like a waterfall, yet it was so gentle and so loving.

He took me into His arms and we began to dance together. For the first time I looked down at myself and saw that I was wearing a wedding gown. He placed His fingers through a loop to hold up the train of the dress and we danced and we danced and we danced. I was weightless in His arms – the arms of my Beloved. When I glanced down at the floor on which we were dancing, I could see that it was made of pure gold, but as transparent as glass. I experienced such love, such forgiveness and such a belonging. He was my Bridegroom and I was His Bride. How I long to be in that place again. How I long for Heaven to invade earth. To this day, I constantly long to be in the arms of my beloved Bridegroom.

The next morning when I awoke in the ministry room at the Church I was surprised to find I still did not have complete control of my body due to the weightiness of the Presence of Holy Spirit upon me. It was very difficult to do ordinary things, such as go home for a shower and drive back to the Church for business as usual.

Although I had no idea at the time what he meant, the guest speaker's declaration that I would 'be like this for many days,' was correct. Alan had to take over many of my usual household duties because my limbs just wouldn't function normally. One of my neighbours thought I had become an alcoholic because I was so unsteady on my feet!

Even though I continued with Prayer Ministry and teaching in the College it was as though I was still living in the Heavenly realm while trying to function here on earth. Also, the Presence I carried was contagious. Anyone who came too close to me came under the same power and had to move away in order to function normally. One day our Pastor sat down to have coffee with us, but when he began to be overcome by the Presence he stood up to leave, saying he had better go now because he had a busy day ahead of him! The Pastor was concerned that this was still happening after three and a half weeks, so he telephoned the guest speaker who had prophesied over me and asked him to seek God as to when my condition would change. The speaker rang back later to say it would last thirty days and then it would be manageable.

On the morning of the thirty first day I woke up feeling strange. I realised the weight of God's Presence had lifted off me and I appeared to be back to 'normal.' However, I was broken hearted, feeling that God had left me. I had a really low time for a few days and then God spoke to me saying *'My precious child, I have not left you. You are no longer feeling the weight of My Glory, but nothing has changed. I am still with you and you are carrying My Presence just the same, without the weighty feeling'*. Relief and then joy filled my soul.

Chapter 10
THE ENEMY STRIKES AGAIN

Soon after these incredible heavenly encounters, pastors from other states began contacting us, requesting to see us privately rather than at the Church where we and the team functioned. They had heard reports of the effectiveness of our ministry and desired personal ministry, but because they were people in leadership they preferred some privacy. We were honoured they had also been told that Alan and I were people of integrity and could be trusted with whatever they shared with us.

Mavis, an Australian missionary on furlough from Indonesia, contacted me. Mavis founded and ran a program in that country to care for disadvantaged and abused women. She invited Alan and me to Indonesia to teach and minister to her staff and to the women in the houses of refuge. She requested we bring a team with us and be prepared to preach in local churches during that time. We promised we would seek God as to whether or not it was His will for us. To our amazement we discovered it was an invitation from the heart of God, with a promise to supply all the finance required. Once again we were stepping out into new territory. We kept our senior Pastor informed and he backed us one hundred percent. The news spread and most of the congregation was excited about what the Lord had opened up for us and our team.

Unfortunately, not everybody was supportive of this new venture. There were some very negative responses which resulted in ungodly rumours. Ministry in Indonesia was put on hold and what followed was a season of dishonour which was extremely painful for all of us.

Eventually, this caused unrest within our formerly loyal and supportive team, and led to a confrontation between myself and the senior Pastor. It became obvious that Alan and I would have to resign from that church. The dilemma we then faced was what would happen to the Prayer Ministry team? What would happen to Christian Counselling College?

We called a meeting at our home with all the team members to explain that we were leaving the church and that the Prayer Ministry and Christian Counselling College would be moving to another venue. We assured them they could remain part of the ministry whether they stayed with that church or move to another. Some chose to stay and continued in the Prayer Ministry there. Other team members left and attended other churches while continuing to be part of our Prayer Ministry Team in a new location. They remained faithful to us even through the difficult transition.

At the end of that year, we faced the difficulty of holding the College Graduation outside of a Church. After prayer, mixed with a lot of grief, we chose to hold the Graduation Ceremony dinner in a restaurant. It was a challenge to find a Pastor who knew the ministry to speak at the Ceremony. Our 'fall from grace', as our resignation became known, adversely influenced many who had once supported and promoted us.

Finally, I approached a leader of a church located in the heart of the city. He willingly agreed to see us. I unloaded from my heart the fallout between us and our former church and asked him if, despite this, he would consider speaking at our Graduation Ceremony in the restaurant. I assured him I would understand if he was to refuse. He agreed without hesitation, saying he knew us well enough to want to honour our ministry. He had known from the outset that it was a call of God on our lives, not mere self-promotion. Alan and I wept with relief. After months of trying to stay positive in the midst of adversity it was re-assuring to have the call of God on our lives affirmed and honoured.

The Graduation Ceremony and Dinner was a memorable experience, perhaps because it was less formal than those which had been held within a church building. Students enjoyed a more open sharing of their personal stories and of their college experiences. As I glanced around the tables at their joyful faces, my heart was blessed.

Part way through the following year there was yet another fallout within the Prayer Ministry Team. I was still fragile from the last incident and I didn't handle this latest one as well as I could have. I simply couldn't take any more. Even though many people chose to dismiss the old rumours and honour us and the ministry, our reputation was still damaged in some circles. We decided to close down at the end of that year.

We asked God why this had happened to a ministry that had been so successful for so long. He showed us that the enemy was furiously opposed to us because there were hundreds of people being healed and restored and going on to assist others. With the Kingdom of God advancing in this way, satan had unleashed a spirit of jealousy against us. With God's help we were able to identify and deal with that door that had been opened in the spirit realm. Looking back, I am now sure that having done that we could have moved on and continued, but I was so discouraged I still chose to close down.

Being hurt for a second time by our own hand-picked team caused much confusion and heartache. Alan seemed to be managing, but I wasn't. I didn't know who I could trust anymore and, even worse, I couldn't hear God in it. It was such a dark place and I realised I would have to do something to get my mind off where I was trapped, climb out of the 'pit', and move on.

At the time my daughter, Cheryl, was a Nutrimetics Consultant. She suggested selling Nutrimetics cosmetics would give me something else to do and keep my mind occupied - a case of telling me to follow my own advice to others! So I became a consultant, conducting cosmetic demonstrations in private homes. I found myself enjoying it. My business grew and prospered and I began receiving awards, including top sales and top recruiting for the month. My daughter was so proud of me.

I'm sure the secret to my success was a good sense of humour and making sure everyone had a great time. Being a teacher by profession, and in ministry, I was equipped to make presentations and answer questions comfortably. I began to enjoy life once again. I still struggled on the spiritual side of my life, but I was slowly recovering from the unjustness which caused Alan and me to close the Prayer Ministry and Counselling College.

A door opened for me to conduct Nutrimetics Shows in the Booleroo Centre area where I had been a teacher. This escalated my sales and the number of shows I ran each month. There was a good reason why these country shows were so successful. I realised that there was nowhere conveniently close where women could purchase cosmetics (there was no such thing as online shopping in those days) and the social aspect was a bonus. Even though I didn't join Nutrimetics with the aim of climbing the success ladder, it happened anyway. I graduated from one level to the next very quickly and soon became a Sales Manager with the offer of a new car - mine for as long as my achievements remained at that level.

And then God told me it was time to give up Nutrimetics because it had served His purpose. Having enjoyed the work so much there was an initial sense of disappointment, but I recognized God had restored my soul while I was selling cosmetics. Restoration of self-esteem, self-worth and self-confidence had dealt with the disappointment and injustice of false accusations and the loss of the ministry. But I had no idea what else He had in mind for me.

Mavis, the missionary in Indonesia, re-established contact. When would I be free to teach Prayer Ministry and preach in the local Churches, there? I explained what had occurred and that we were no longer in ministry and had the disapproval of many. Mavis's response was that she didn't care about any of that because God had told her to invite us to minister. Alan and I promised her we would seek God as well as speak to some of the team who were still available.

Mavis gave us a brochure containing all the aspects of Mission Uplift's Social Project and we read it prayerfully. The Mission's foundation scripture, *'A new commandment I give to you that you love one another. As I have loved you so must you love one another. By this all men shall know that you are My disciples, if you love one another.'* **(John 13:34-35)** had led them to establish refuges, orphanages, kindergartens, rehabilitation centres. a hotline and crisis centre, and a cafe.

Many of the women - some as young as fourteen - are victims of enforced prostitution and rape, resulting in unwanted pregnancies. Under Muslim law this incurs death by stoning. Regardless of their situation, God loves them, and Mavis saw the need to express that love in practical ways. Hundreds of babies have been born into the program, cared for by a foundation set up by Mavis. The mothers stay at the centre for forty days following the birth, giving time for counselling and prayer ministry.

Alan and I were touched so deeply by what we were reading that we immediately began to sponsor an Indonesian child. I continue sponsoring to this day.

God eventually made it plain that it was His will that we accept Mavis' invitation to take a team to Indonesia. We began to make preparations.

The first challenge was to know which team members God wanted us to take with us. We needed a team with the flexibility to teach as well as prayer minister. Having been assured of God's choices we approached each one individually. Their initial responses were almost identical: 'Who me?' They were amazed that the Lord would ask them to be part of this mission. They set themselves to seek God diligently as to His will and purpose for their involvement. All of them agreed to be part of this assignment.

None of us was in a position to pay air fees and other expenses so each of us sought God for His provision. God was true to His Word to supply our every need. He provided for each one of us individually, and in totally different and supernatural ways. There was more than enough to cover all of our costs with money left over to leave a financial blessing to those in need in Indonesia.

Mavis gave us a list of things to remember while we were in Indonesia so that we did not fall out of favour by offending cultural conventions. Some of those things were:

- Don't touch people's heads in a playful or disrespectful way. It is okay to lay hands on a person's head while praying.
- Don't give or take anything with your left hand (this was extremely difficult for Jean who was left-handed).
- When accompanying an Indonesian always assume they do not have money. Buy for the Indonesian person, too, if you are buying a drink, ice-cream or other food for yourself. Do not ask if they would like a drink etc, because they will never say 'yes'. If you invite a person to eat with you, you will be expected to pay. If they invite you, they will pay.

- Both men and women outside of the home are expected to wear clothing with sleeves. No bare shoulders. No miniskirts.
- Indonesians care about appearance so bring suitable clothing for Church and meetings. When preaching men must wear ties, and women must wear skirt and blouse, or dress, not trousers.
- When given food always try to eat at least some of it. It is acceptable to leave some as this is considered polite.
- Be friendly. Never complain about food or conditions you may have to live in. Remember you are only in Indonesia for a short time, so accept the conditions provided even though you find them difficult. It is not Australia, so don't expect it to be the same as home.
- Do not give your name and address to anyone unless you are prepared to be pestered by people with letters asking for money and other things. Before giving anything always ask the missionary if it is wise. There are always those who will feed you a good story, while others who genuinely could do with help go without.
- Do not flash money around. There are many pick-pockets, but there also many needy people who may be tempted if you are careless.
- Be careful when dealing with the opposite sex. An evening alone or time spent in a secluded place could mean an enforced wedding to save face.
- It is helpful to know some Indonesian phrases such as 'good morning,' 'good afternoon,' 'good evening,' 'good night,' 'thank you,' 'praise the Lord' etc. People will take you into their heart if they know you bothered to learn a few words of their language. Purchase an Indonesian dictionary and get a head start before arriving in Indonesia

Many of these challenged us, along with having to adjust to teaching and preaching through interpreters. We gathered a prayer team who diligently prayed for us as we prepared for this, our first mission trip. They also agreed to meet together on a regular basis to pray for us until we returned. We were so grateful for the commitment of these prayer warriors.

The months of preparation flew by. There was so much to do and learn, but God was faithful to help us so that we did not fall behind in our tight schedule. During this time we felt to change the name of our ministry from 'Living Springs' to 'Fresh Wine International'. Hand in hand with Holy Spirit, it was a new season and a fresh start.

As our departure date grew closer we were surprised to discover that rather than feeling nervous we all had a sense of excitement. It came as a confirmation that we were right in the will of God, individually and as a team. We were conscious of His favour on every aspect of preparation.

Chapter 11
THE DOOR TO INDONESIA OPENS

All was in place. I had written all my conference material, updated our Prayer Ministry Training and prepared my sermons. More importantly, all of us had prepared our hearts to remain open and obedient vessels for God to flow through to touch the hearts of Indonesian people.

The great day arrived. Jean and Muriel were already at the airport before us, along with over a dozen of our team to pray for us. Then Muriel, who had emigrated from England with her husband, discovered that her entry visa would expire before our return to Australia. She was informed she would not be allowed to re-enter Australia unless she applied for the visa to be updated in Bali. None of us had any doubt that Muriel was part of God's plan for us in Indonesia, so she opted to attend to the visa in Bali on the way home. Fortunately, arrival and departure were from Bali because there were no direct flights to Yogyakarta where we were ministering.

It was an uncomfortably hot hour or more at Bali airport as we were processed through customs and changed our money into local currency. That discomfort turned out to be mild compared to the hour and a half drive in the van to Solo. It was a scary drive because there didn't appear to be any road rules. It was the survival of the fittest, or perhaps the bravest! Even the pedestrians had no rights. They waited for a break in traffic and then ran like mad for the other side. On the arrival at the house where we were to stay, Mavis broke the news to us that she had to return to Australia in two days time, as she had been called back to attend to an urgent matter, which could not be postponed. One of the orphanage leaders and another couple came for tea during which Mavis talked about her final plans and made arrangements for us to be cared for. Mavis was the only person we knew in Indonesia at that point, so it was quite unsettling for us to be left in the hands of total strangers most of whom could not speak English.

Within forty eight hours Mavis had departed. Two of her staff broke down, weeping over the situation and the future of the ministry. Even though they could not understand what we were saying, Muriel and I prayed for them to experience God's comfort. We knew how they felt. It was an awkward situation for us, too.

We spent the rest of the day going over our notes, listening to worship music and praying for the Seminar. In the evening we packed what was needed for the four day staff retreat being held in the mountains, a distance of two hour's drive. We went through many interesting little towns and the scenery was stunning. We had never seen so many people in one place.

The retreat venue was a place of great beauty with well-cared for gardens and a peaceful atmosphere. It was as if God had arrived before us! However our bunk beds had been made for very thin people, and the toilet and shower area was a culture shock. We were very conscious of Mavis's instruction not to comment on the differences from Australian conditions! We were relieved to meet our interpreter, Eva, and to communicate in English.

After a light meal with staff it was time for the first session of the four-day Prayer Ministry Seminar. For each of us teaching (Muriel, Jean and myself) it was our first experience of teaching through an interpreter, but Eva was an experienced interpreter so we found it reasonably easy to make the adjustment. We taught a morning session, two in the afternoon, and one evening session, followed by an excellent worship time.

On day two of the Seminar I taught on 'Rejection' and the practical turned into an anointed ministry time. The Presence of Jesus was tangible and there was much healing and restoration. When Muriel completed the teaching on 'Repentance' Holy Spirit came upon us in a mighty way and the whole group went into an unplanned time of intercession for the nation of Indonesia. Led by Holy Spirit, high level intercession flowed. The people cried out for their nation, repenting for generational iniquities, and God manifested Himself powerfully. When Jean spoke on 'Generational Iniquities' and led the practical session, there was wild rejoicing as many were being set free.

We were pleased that God had given us the idea to include some visuals to accompany our teaching. For example, when we spoke about the necessity of receiving healing for the soul we had a volunteer wrapped in grave clothes, to represent Lazarus. He lay on the floor and I called to him to arise. Then, as Jesus did, I commanded others to unwrap the grave clothes. This represents God speaking life to us (being born again) through His Spirit, and then other Christians bringing healing and restoration to the hurting, broken areas of the soul. It was a vivid and appropriate way to illustrate many of the areas taught in the Seminar and brought many to repentance and emotional healing.

At the conclusion of the four-day Seminar there was a presentation time where each of us on the teaching team were thanked and given gifts. Those giving thanks, including some of the pastors and leaders, shed tears of gratitude. It had been a special time of the Spirit moving amongst us and we found it hard to say goodbye.

The next day, we were at the first Church where I was to preach. God was gracious to provide me with a young interpreter who was so enthusiastic in his interpretation. Later, he told me the message so impacted him as to bring something alive in him. Many others responded to the altar call and were deeply touched by God.

God's awesome Presence in that place was the topic of conversation as we were driven to the next Church where I was to preach. Once again, the Presence of God was powerful. I am sure it was the passion and hunger in the people that drew God's Presence in such a mighty way. Again, the response to the altar call was enthusiastic. God poured out His Spirit upon them as they knelt crying out for more of Him. There was a hunger and humility that I had not yet witnessed in Australia.

After such a full-on morning the team was grateful for a relaxed afternoon and a free evening in which to review my material for the teaching session in Solo Bible College the next day.

Both the Pastor and the students were noticeably moved as I shared about the work of Holy Spirit in counselling. Lasting freedom is only achieved when the Spirit of God reveals what needs to be dealt with in a person's life. The Pastor came back to Mavis' place with us and we talked for hours. So much of what we take for granted in Australia was a fresh revelation to him. He was a thirsty sponge, soaking up every word. He invited me to speak at his Church the following Sunday and to teach several more lessons in the 'Christian Counselling' class in the Bible College during the week. He asked if we would consider coming back the following year to conduct a seminar on 'Listening to God's Voice'.

A local Pastor and his wife took us on a tour of the Solo Crisis Centre where, later, we would be conducting a four day Seminar on 'Healing and Restoration'. This centre housed unmarried mothers-to-be. These young women were genuinely grateful for being rescued from being stoned. Their dear, uplifted faces pulled at our heart strings. The centre was set up to cater for them and their babies to stay for a period of time until they decided on their baby's future. It is hard to decide whether to accept its adoption, leave it in the orphanage, or raise the child themselves. The girls were given vital information on each of these choices but it had to be their own personal choice. Many of them were so young to be having to make that decision, knowing they would have to live with it the rest of their life.

Following the tour of the Crisis Centre we were taken to the local Christian Bookshop. I purchased a framed picture of the Lion of the Tribe of Judah which is still displayed in my lounge room to this day. It is a constant reminder not only of our first trip to Indonesia, but also that Jesus Christ is both the Lamb of God and the Lion. Of course, we did not purchase books because we could hardly speak a word of Indonesian, let alone read it. We did purchase gifts for those who were taking care of us - the drivers, housemaids, cooks. The list was long, because we were treated like royalty everywhere we went.

The following day, Sunday, it was 'preaching as usual'. After preaching at Pastor Jocko's Church, we were invited to his home where his wife, Joyce, provided our lunch. The meal was really great, but the time of fellowship was even greater. All the Indonesian pastors we had met to date were so hungry for more of the presence and power of God in their lives.

We visited both the Palace and the Museum in the afternoon and then attended the evening Church service on the Bible College campus. It was at the Bible College, during the week, that Muriel, Jean and I taught our course, 'Listening to the Voice of God'. On the final day there was time for testimonies from those who had been ministered to during the Seminar. There were many tears as they shared how God had touched their lives. Pastors were weeping, we were weeping, and there was much praise to God for moving in such a powerful, personal way in their lives.

It was an early morning departure for Bali, to enable Muriel to attend to her re-entry visa into Australia. Praise God, it was all taken care of within half an hour at the Australian Consulate. We went off with light hearts to lunch at the hotel ahead of a bus trip to a local village where the mood was very different. There were beggars everywhere. The poverty of the people was very visible. At one point we felt unsafe because we realised we were being followed. We hailed a taxi to take us back to our hotel.

The next morning we planned to shop for gifts for friends and family, but after our experience the day before, we paid our taxi driver to accompany us and bargain on our behalf so we could enjoy the markets in safety. Later that day we boarded for our long flight back to Australia. We knew we would never forget the people we had met and ministered to. Indeed, we returned to minister in Indonesia several times over the next eighteen years.

The second time we took a team to Indonesia proved to be even more eventful than the first. We began by attending the wedding of one of the orphans. What an occasion for celebration! How wonderful it was to see the young groom, raised in the orphanage, being united with his beautiful bride, and starting a new chapter in his life.

Our first preaching assignment was at a Church near the Bible College campus where we were billeted. After this meeting I was approached by a leader of another church called the Roadside Chapel. He explained that it ministered to street people in a dangerous area and even arriving in a car we would be harassed. I accepted his invitation despite the risks. Hadn't I just preached in a Church building with open sides, with a military man on a motorbike driving back and forth outside with a gun in his hand? I decided that there surely couldn't be a better way to die than preaching the gospel! We survived to preach again at the evening service and minister to many for healing and deliverance.

But I was tested when we arrived at the Roadside Chapel. People were banging on the car, holding their hands out for money and we were harassed all the way from the car to the building which housed the one-room Chapel. Everybody, including Alan, me and the team, sat on a cement floor covered with plastic sheeting. Not the most comfortable for us westerners, but the amazing worship was so wonderful we forgot the seating. The street people praised and worshipped so passionately. After the preaching they responded enthusiastically to my altar call for salvation and healing. There were some amazing healing miracles. They were more hungry for the things of God than for food. It was an experience I will never forget.

Ministering to the children in the orphanage was a privilege indeed. Jean preached the Word of God and seven children gave their hearts to the Lord Jesus. This was followed by prayer for healing and deliverance, during which several children experienced miraculous healing and one young girl was delivered from an evil spirit. She had been sold to satan by her own father who was a witch doctor. Even after her father died she was tormented by his voice calling to her. Once she was delivered from witchcraft the voice immediately stopped and she was free.

There were several further opportunities to minister to the children and staff at the orphanage. More children were saved, others healed physically, some delivered and quite a number healed in their souls. This, of course, is very often the root of mental, physical and emotional problems. Those orphans had suffered much damage from the circumstances of their birth and consequent upbringing. Our loving Heavenly Father had such compassion for them and many were healed and restored.

I could write a whole book just on our ministry trips to Indonesia, but I will limit myself to a few highlights. We were constantly amazed by the deliverance of children. There was often witchcraft in their family lines which hindered their walk with God, especially for those who hungered for a more intimate relationship with

Jesus and Father God. I particularly remember one lady who had been dedicated to satan in a ritualistic ceremony in her childhood. But nothing is too difficult for God. She was set totally free from bondage to satan and healed of all the wounds to her soul. To see her countenance change as Jesus set her free was most encouraging to us as a team.

On a different trip, we were teaching on intercession when we were asked to lead the group in prayer for the country's imminent government election. There was great division and warfare of words between the candidates. We asked for an Indonesian flag to be brought into the meeting. Everyone held a part of it as we cried out for unity and peace in the country during the elections. As we boarded the flight from Solo back to Jakarta we were handed a newspaper in the English language in which we read an article entitled 'The Race Begins'. There was a photo with the caption, 'presidential and vice presidential candidates gather together on stage in a show of unity to mark the beginning of the election campaign'. All candidates had signed a plaque saying 'Ready to accept victory or defeat'. This had never happened before. God is the God of the miraculous!

On one ministry trip we held three tent meetings in three days, which was quite a challenge for us given the heat and humidity. But with the help of Holy Spirit we Aussies coped well and there were some remarkable results. Many, people were saved, healed and set free from bondages. The Spirit of God was evident, with signs, wonders and miracles following. During that outpouring quite a number of the people were filled with Holy Spirit and began speaking in tongues. These results dispelled all pre-service apprehension.

In 2011, Alan and I received an invitation to Andrew's wedding which was to be held in Bali during one of our missions to Indonesia. You will remember that Andrew was the child I had surrendered to adoption during my marriage to Lyall. After consulting with the trip organiser we were granted 48 hours leave to fly to Bali from Jakarta to attend the wedding. We were so thankful to our team for filling our commitments in our absence, because the wedding was to prove very special. At this our first ever meeting, Andrew's parents embraced me, and Alan too, as if we were their closest friends. Adopting Andrew had brought them such fulfilment and pleasure. They told us they had diligently prayed for Andrew's birth mother knowing she would have suffered in giving up her child, regardless of the circumstances. Their compassion brought tears to my eyes. It was an experience I will never forget.

As we prepared to fly back to Australia after this mission we enjoyed an early breakfast with Mavis and spent time at the Orphanage saying goodbye to staff and children before departing for the airport. Jakarta Airport was a scary place that day. The atmosphere seemed to be heavy with something evil. We were unable to get any details but there was a heavy security presence, few westerners, and we attracted uncomfortable attention. It was a relief to board our flight to Singapore and finally arrive safely in Adelaide.

One particular year as we were waiting on God for our Seminar topics and sermons, I had a vision of a huge lion roaring over a map of Indonesia. This vision remained with me for weeks so I sought God for clarification. I described to an artist friend what I'd seen in the Spirit and she agreed to paint the lion onto a banner, insisting she knew exactly what the lion looked like. I was sceptical, but when I collected the finished banner the lion was exactly what I had seen. The Lord showed us that He, the Lion of the Tribe of Judah, was going to roar over Indonesia. He told me I was to wave this banner only when He directed me to do so. I sensed this would be at times when His authority would manifest in my life as never before.

That year, the teaching session on Spiritual Warfare was followed by student participation in a practical demonstration. When all hell broke loose in the place I expected to hear God instruct me to wave the banner, but He didn't. Instead, a break-through anointing erupted and there were major deliverances. When I prayed for the break-through anointing to fall upon all the participants, Heaven came down. The power and Presence of God in the room that night was unforgettable.

There was also a powerful Presence of the Lord at the three-day Revival Meetings. Several people, including a Muslim girl, gave their lives to the Lord, two rededicated their lives and many were healed and delivered. On the third evening, after the teaching, God instructed me to wave the Lion banner. The people went wild under the power of God and there was a wave of miraculous healings, people saved and infilling of Holy Spirit. The many personal testimonies at the end of the meeting were amazing. To God, alone, be all the glory.

On yet another trip I had preached on God's Grace at an 8.00 am service and spent the afternoon preparing my sermon for the evening meeting at the same church. As we stepped out of the car on arrival, there was a torrential downpour. We entered the building totally drenched. In a side room, we removed and squeezed the water out of our clothing as best we could before putting them back on to go into the meeting. My hair was messy, my clothing barely presentable. God was dealing with any and all traces of pride!

I spoke on abandonment. At the altar call, grown men rolled on the floor, yelling as the pain of abandonment was released. Women and young girls wept as they were released and filled with God's love. Then the Lord gave me the following word for the pastor: 'Look around and see. This Church is a hospital – a place where I will bind up broken hearts and set captives free. I am raising up a strong Church filled with those who are healed and whole on the 'inside' who will be able to bring healing and restoration to others.' Receiving this word, the pastor fell on his knees and asked us to pray for him. I anointed him with oil and prayed. Later, he told us his Church had never experienced such anointed ministry and that the word from God had answered his heart cry.

Following a week of Seminars on another trip when I preached on the Sunday evening, God's presence so filled the place it felt like Heaven came down. Any need we prayed for was met: healing, deliverance, more of Holy Spirit, restoration of the soul. Heaven opened over us and our requests were answered immediately.

The following day, on the same trip, I spoke to children at a seminar on the Love of God. I gave each of them red cardboard hearts with a black dot in the middle, depicting a hole in our heart. After sharing how much God loved them, I handed out little white hearts to stick over the black hole in the red heart, explaining that God's pure love fills that black emptiness. I prayed for the children to ask Jesus to come into their hearts and invited them to come to the front if they wanted Jesus to be Saviour and Lord. Nearly all of them responded.

It's hard to reduce eighteen wonderful years to a few short pages. It's even harder to convey the privilege of teaching and ministering into the lives of children and adults in Indonesia, or to describe the awesome provision of God in it all. I might just add here that never once did Alan and I, or any other team member, have to pay our own air fares and accommodation. That was God's doing, too. Without us telling any human being what was required, God always provided the finance. We always prayed that finance would come as confirmation that it was God's will to go each time. Ahead of one particular trip, during a time of prayer together for financial confirmation, we had a call from the husband of a lady who used to be on our team. He asked if we were going to Indonesia any time soon. Determined not to tell him we were praying into the next trip, I asked 'What makes you ask?' He told me that God had asked him to send us a cheque for $10,000.00. Now this was the exact amount needed for five of us to travel. Only God knew we would not need money for six. Alan became ill and did not travel with us on that occasion. God is faithful!

Chapter 12
ALAN'S PROMOTION TO GLORY

Early in 2010 we faced another challenge when Alan was diagnosed with prostate cancer. I am not a lover of challenges. It's true that the only thing that makes them acceptable is that 'anything the enemy means for evil God always turns around for good'. God is always faithful to His word.

Alan came through the first surgery with flying colours. The specialist surgeon announced that all the cancer had been removed and Alan should have a full recovery. Cause for celebration, indeed! He was cancer-free for two years, during which we made another ministry trip to Indonesia and continued to build Fresh Wine International.

Then the cancer recurred. The next three and half years were spent in continual operations, and chemo treatments. When Alan was hospitalised I spent five hours every day at his side. One morning I was driving to the hospital and stopped at the traffic lights at a city intersection. I woke up to find other drivers tooting me. I had fallen asleep behind the wheel – a 'micro-nap'. It was scary to wonder what would have happened if my foot had slipped off the brake in those few seconds. My team decided that for the time being I should not be driving into the city each day. They arranged a roster so that someone drove me to the hospital in the morning and another picked me up five hours later. The team of volunteer drivers included a number of pastors, all willing to help for a long as necessary.

I will never forget the day when one of the pastors drove me home. When he asked me how I was coping, I confessed it was difficult to accept that people were needing to fit my transport into their own busy schedules. Now we all know that pastors give sermons on Sundays, but that day I learned they can give them anywhere, even on the side of the road! He pulled over and preached the best one sentence sermon I ever heard on 'Receiving'. He asked me what I got out of giving. Because giving gives me much pleasure I went to great lengths to explain the joy of blessing others, etc. 'Well stop robbing mine,' was his reply. I got it.

I received further help to make sure I got a handle on that revelation. When Alan was at home, and looking after him made my schedule more hectic, the team arranged a roster for friends and Church members to bring an evening meal each day. One evening as I walked to the door thanking a lady for her lovely meal, I found myself saying to God under my breath, 'I can't handle this.' He replied, 'Have you considered that this is Me demonstrating my love for you through these kind people?' I had to be honest: it hadn't even crossed my mind. This forever changed my perspective on receiving. In fact, I have used these two testimonies to teach on the subject. It's been a revelation to many.

Another challenge while Alan was in hospital was when I injured myself during my early morning walk. Apparently, I didn't lift my feet high enough on an uneven patch and landed heavily. My head hurt, there was a lot of pain in one arm and I was unable to get up. I phoned my neighbours and they moved me into their home and called an ambulance.

Ambulance officers completed their initial assessment and told me the protocol was for me to be taken to the local hospital. I didn't want to go there because Alan was in a city hospital. I explained that if they couldn't take me to St. Andrews, where Alan was, I would arrange for friends to transport me. Fortunately, the officers obtained permission to break protocol.

After x-rays were taken, it was established I had a broken elbow and facial injuries. My face was so bruised I was unrecognisable. I was worried about the effect this might have on Alan when I was allowed to go to his room for my normal daily visit. I decided to ring him first, and told him my appearance was worse than the injuries, but in spite of my protests a porter wheeled-chaired me to Alan's room. Alan was shocked. I had not realised the bruising had continued to spread and become much darker. However, my famous sense of humour came to the rescue and my jokes about my face allayed Alan's anxiety.

Due to Alan being in and out of St Andrews Hospital, we established a warm relationship with the Chaplain. Alan's private room seemed to be his favourite spot in the hospital. In fact, staff and visitors often commented about the great atmosphere created by a combination of humour, love and the presence of God. I loved being there, too. What a long way God had brought me - from the trash heap where He found me, to an appreciation of His presence and able to show His love to the hurt and broken.

After five and a half years of struggle Alan's suffering was unbearable. Jason (Alan's son) and I realised he was only clinging to life for my sake. We discussed this and decided we needed to release him to go to Jesus whenever he was ready. In response to me telling him that, he looked me straight in the eyes and asked, 'Will you be alright financially?' I was touched by his care, but managed to restrain my tears and answer, 'Yes, I'll be fine.' He seemed to breathe a sigh of relief and relaxed.

Two mornings later the hospital called me to say Alan had deteriorated dramatically and I should come to the hospital immediately. Jason and Cheryl joined me there and we were able to hold his hand and love on him until he was promoted to glory a few hours later.

We celebrated his life at a funeral that was filled with real life humorous stories, testimonies of what God had done in us individually and as a couple in ministry. There was a reverence for a life well lived. Two different guests, both sitting in different places in the chapel saw a portal open into heaven, with Jesus and a smiling Alan, looking down at the service. The funeral directors told us it was the best service they had been privileged to conduct.

A few weeks later, just as I was waking up, I looked up to see a white screen opening up in front of me. I watched in wonder as Jesus and Alan appeared on the screen walking together in a most beautiful garden. As they passed by, Alan turned briefly in my direction and said, 'Hi honey, I'm fine and Heaven is just like you told me it would be'. He was so happy and well. I was a bit miffed at his quick glance and few words, but after meditating upon it I realised that He so enjoyed being with Jesus that earthly things were no longer important to him. However, the few words he spoke were significant. Every time I had visited him in hospital, he always greeted me with, "Hi honey,' and when I asked him how he was, he always replied, 'I'm fine.' I was reminded, too, that in the last months of his life he often asked me to share again my experience of going to Heaven. These things settled me and confirmed my inner knowing that He was in heaven for eternity with His Lord and Saviour, Jesus Christ.

Several months later I remembered the Chaplain of St Andrews who had been most supportive and encouraging. Thinking to support others as he had done for us, I had an urge to take on a role as Chaplain. I contacted him and shared what I was considering. He said I would make a good Chaplain, but suggested I ask God what my motives were for desiring to be a Chaplain. I did this, expecting God would tell me it was because of my desire to help others, but to my surprise His response was, 'You are looking to do this because you are bored and lonely!' That shocked me! However, it didn't take long for me to acknowledge the truth of it.

Grieving is different for everybody. I was having to make enormous adjustments. Alan and I had done everything together. We had birthed the ministry, trained prayer ministry teams and established the Christian Counselling College. No two people are alike in the way we handle situations, but I remembered that I had counselled many over the years to take two years to really work through the grieving process. I needed to 'practice what I'd preached'. The next two years were very difficult. Losing a loved one is a never easy. Just living alone is hard to adjust to, not to mention managing finances and other practical things. But God was so faithful to me, and during those two years I entered into an increased intimacy with Him which I still enjoy today.

One of the most valuable lessons I learned in this journey was being absolutely real in my relationship with God. I am a person of reality and I had found that just saying to God 'I trust you' in circumstances didn't do it for me. I began to reword my statement to, 'Lord I am choosing to trust You – Holy Spirit would you please make that a reality'. I am sure God honoured the humility and I found I could trust Him completely. I soon began to use this re-wording in many other situations, such as **'Father God, I choose to forgive . . . Holy Spirit would you please make this a reality'**. I have taught this to many people who have come for Prayer Ministry and it has been life-changing for them, too.

God faithfully met my every need. About three months after Alan changed his address to Heaven I remember looking up at the ceiling and wondering what I was going to do about the ducted air conditioning. It was quite old and we had to have it fixed nearly every year before summer. I did not pray – it was just a 'wondering.' Within a few days I received a letter from England. As an emigrant to Australia, Alan had an English part-pension, so I had to notify them of his death. The letter was in response to that. It informed me that the Department had been checking through Alan's paperwork and discovered that he had been underpaid for over twelve years and that I was entitled to almost ten thousand English pounds. 'If it sounds too good to be true, it probably is' was my first thought, but I kept reading. The last paragraph read, 'if we do not hear from you within three months, this amount will automatically be placed into your bank account'. A$15,000.00 was duly placed into my bank account and was enough to pay for brand new ducted air conditioning and finalise the funeral account. Did God care for me? Unconditionally - in every single area. He meets every need.

A few months before the end of the two years grieving time, I received an invitation from Mavis to speak at an international event in Indonesia when she would hand her work over to a younger woman. She reminded me that I had prophesied over her several years earlier that this would happen, even though she did not receive the word at the time. Because of this she really wanted me to be the speaker, and believed it was God's direction.

As I pondered this invitation, I realised that the two years I had set for myself was not set in concrete, but rather a guideline to work through the passing of a loved one. I sought God for His plan and purpose for this occasion and He showed me very clearly that this was in His plan for my life at this time.

Chapter 13
FINAL TRIP TO INDONESIA

I considered what it meant to hand over a mantle to another person, and the appropriate way to do this. I took into account that it would not take place in Australia, but in Indonesia where cultural rules are quite different.

Handing over a God-given mantle is of incredible spiritual significance. In handing God's calling and anointing to the next person of God's choice, it is vitally important to hear accurately who He has chosen and the right time for it to take place. After researching Indonesian cultural protocols and Biblical examples of handing over mantles, Mavis and I came up with what we believed was God's way of doing it. There was a special mantle designed and made which Mavis would wear over her shoulders at the ceremony. After a short message which the Lord gave me, I would remove the mantle from Mavis who would then place it on the new leader's shoulders. Because Indonesian culture designates the man as the person of authority in the family, we included the husband in the ceremony too. The Lord's strategy for this was to hand a baton to him as part of the ceremony.

Exactly seven days before I was to fly to Indonesia I was hit by the enemy so violently I had to be taken to hospital by ambulance. X-rays revealed I had broken my coccyx bone. On being released from hospital, I was advised I should not fly to Indonesia the following weekend. I explained I could not be replaced at such short notice and would meet my commitment whether they approved or not. Unsuccessful in talking me out of that, they instructed me to take regular, short walks in the aisle during the flight.

The night before boarding the flight the pain was so intense I could not sleep. I was grateful Alan's son, Jason, arrived early to drive me to the airport, and helped me with all those last minute chores and packing the car; the things Alan would have done for me. There had been few occasions when Alan had not accompanied me in ministry and I missed him in so many ways.

Mavis, along with her daughter and granddaughter, met me in Adelaide and we enjoyed a coffee and chat before going through the boarding procedures and departing for Sydney. Only after we transferred to our international flight did I realise the support cushion for my injury had been left on the plane from Adelaide. It was almost an hour before one of the Qantas staff finally located it and brought it to me just in time to board the flight to Jakarta. How grateful I would be for that little cushion - I had no idea just how agonising the journey would be. Three hours into the flight, my body went into meltdown – freezing, involuntary shaking, loss of focus etc. It was a horrific experience. I arrived in Jakarta in a state of shock and endured a restless night.

The next day one of the visitors to the handover celebration prayed for my healing and the pain became manageable. In the following days I attempted some shopping and sight-seeing with Mavis, but there was no further healing and I began to question whether I should have listened to medical advice and not come to Indonesia. Where was God in all this? He gave me the following word:

> *'My child, be still, be still. I have not left you.*
> *I am right here, right now, in this place with you.*
> *You are not alone. Fear not, for I am with you.*
>
> *It is My plan and purpose for you to be right*
> *here where you are at this particular time.*
> *Though the enemy has raged against you, be*
> *assured My child, you are right in the centre*
> *of My will at this very moment.*

I have called you here to fulfil My plan and purpose and I will back up My plan as only I can.

Walk step by step in faith with expectation of what I will do, for surely My purposes for this hour will be fulfilled, and I will be glorified both in you and through you'.

The handover ceremony and celebration fulfilled all the cultural requirements and was a memorable occasion. It was an emotional time for Mavis. Femme and her husband received the mantle and the baton with true grace and humility which I'm sure is remembered favourably by all who attended. The blessing, presence and power of the Lord were very evident on the day and it was testified to by over three hundred visitors, including local and international pastors.

In the weeks following I gave one-on-one personal prayer ministry, conducted several seminars, and preached in various Churches. Only the Lord could have enabled me to do it. Not only was I battling physical pain but it was the first trip I had taken on my own without even team support. It was a lonely time as memories of Alan triggered my emotions. However, all of that was offset by the outpouring of Holy Spirit as I ministered. I had not witnessed salvations, healings and deliverances to that level, before. People responding to altar calls fell under the power of Holy Spirit even before they reached the altar. God was at work in a mighty and miraculous way. It was an honour and a privilege to co-labour with God in such a dimension.

During one of the Seminars I noticed a young man weeping while I was speaking. At the end of the session he gave a testimony. He shared that God had been speaking to him for quite some time about developing intimacy with Him. He had not understood what God was trying to draw him into, but my teaching had explained what intimacy with Father God meant, and that it was an honour and privilege that He wanted to spend time with us at that deeper level.

There was confirmation from Mavis when she shared that the content of my teaching had been on her heart prior to the seminar. It is always good to receive feedback confirming that we are being led by Him from preparation to presentation.

While preaching in one of the local churches, the Spirit of God came down so powerfully, and many were saved, healed and delivered. One of the leaders told me afterwards that glitter had appeared on my face as I stood to preach and it remained until the end of the service. That's a reminder that it's never about us, but ALL ABOUT HIM!

The flight back to Australia was still quite painful. I wasn't able to rest comfortably for any length of time. It was great to be back in Adelaide and my own home, but even then the pain was still with me. It puzzled me as to why there had not been total healing and restoration. In total frustration I cried out to God, asking "Why, why, why?" He gave me two words, 'Your mouth'. For three weeks I asked Him what He meant by this, but there was no reply. Then, while chatting with a friend about a driver who had cut in front of me that morning, I commented that such drivers are *'a pain in the butt'* - a phrase I often used. The moment those words came out of my mouth I knew what the Lord was trying to teach me through my broken coccyx. Life and death are in the power of the tongue and you get what you say. When I repented of using that expression over many years, the pain left immediately and to this day has never returned.

This was one of the most powerful lessons I have learned concerning healing. We need to be speaking over ourselves the Word of God, not the medical diagnosis or symptoms we are experiencing. What I'd learnt became a valuable help to many others.

When we go through difficult times it is wise to find a Scripture which speaks the positive about our circumstances, and declare it over and over until it becomes a reality. It allows the truth of God's Word to overcome the lies that the enemy uses against us. This applies in every situation: health, finances, family, employment, or whatever. The Word of God is far more powerful than satan's lies. When spoken out loud on a regular basis it will destroy the strongholds he's tried to build in our minds.

Chapter 14
GOD OPENS NEW DOORS FOR MINISTRY

Life was pretty quiet after I returned from the handover celebration in Indonesia. In the first few months I continued to adjust to living a single life and kept a 'low profile' until the two years were up. During this time I reminded the Lord Jesus that all He had taught me in the area of healing and restoration was so valuable it would be good if I could pass it on to others before I changed my address from earth to Heaven. I loved seeing people healed and restored, and their testimonies of changed lives were all the reward I ever needed. I knew the work should continue. God's answer was an invitation to speak at a Women's Conference on Yorke Peninsula in country South Australia.

The title He gave me for the Conference was *"Healing the Soul"*. The morning session explored *'Developing an Intimate Friendship with God'* and after the lunchbreak I shared on *'Restoring our Soul so we can Prosper and be in Health'*. In the first session I shared the difference between *'knowing about'* God and actually *'knowing'* Him. I went back to God's first relationship with man. Imagine walking and talking with God in the garden like Adam and Eve did! God created us for intimate relationship - a walking, talking relationship. Talking together - us speaking to God **and** God speaking to us (do we wait for Him to speak to us, or do we do all the talking?). Walking together - we need to **trust Him** to be able to walk with Him. Relationship is the currency of Heaven. Religion **con**forms - conforms us to a set of rules. Relationship **trans**forms - transforms us into His likeness.

'Busyness' seems to be a way of life these days but the Word of God says, *'Be still and know that I am God'* (Psalm 46:10). This is an absolute key to developing intimacy. Some other key Scriptures are:

> Psalm 27:4 One thing have I desired of that Lord, that will I seek, that I may dwell in the house of the Lord all the days of my life, to behold the beauty of the Lord and to enquire in His temple.
>
> Prov. 8:17 I love those who love me and those who diligently seek Me will find Me.
>
> Philip. 3:10 That I may know God .. progressively become more intimately acquainted with Him, perceiving ... recognising ... understanding ... continually transformed.
>
> Rev. 4:1 Come up here and I will show you things which must take place after this.

Intimacy with the Lord is an ongoing, unfolding experience, having precious fellowship with God, talking heart to heart. When was the last time you asked God what was on His heart rather than telling Him all that is on yours?

Knowing God intimately is the answer to all our problems. Our relationship with the Lord Jesus Christ brings us into divine favour, with access to all God is, and has. Jesus is knocking at the door of our hearts asking to come in. He does not force His way, but patiently knocks. If we open the door in obedience to His voice, He will come in and commune with us. Then He will open the door of Heaven to us. When that happens, we are given Divine insight and breakthrough will come! My continual prayer is,

> 'Lord Jesus, I want to see Your face
> I want to hear Your voice

I want to understand Your ways
and I want to know Your Love'.

At the conclusion of this session God gave me this prophetic word:

"No room, no room"

I am knocking. I am knocking at the door of your hearts. How will you respond to Me? Will you respond as those who responded to Mary and Joseph, 'There is no room; there is no room in the Inn?'

Is there no room in your lives to spend quality time with Me, getting to know Me, sharing your heart with Me, and allowing Me to share My heart with you? I have so much more to reveal to you, My beloved.

If only you could know how I long for your intimate friendship. Oh, how I long to linger with you. My heart yearns for your company. How much longer will your busyness, your insecurities, your doubts and fears keep me knocking at the door of your heart?

Don't allow the law to lock Me out any longer. Open your heart wide and allow us to embrace one another in the relationship I long to have with each of you, My very, very precious children. There is so much more, so much more. My heart longs for you, My friends, with such a deep, deep longing.

Will you respond to Me today? Will you respond to My persistent knocking at the door of your heart and allow Me to be your Best Friend? I desire your friendship. I love you unconditionally and My heart yearns for you - yes, for you!

It tugs at my heart to know that God wants our friendship even more than we want His. How do you respond to that word?

The congregation's response to this word was intense. The altar was packed with weeping women totally undone in the Spirit! During the lunch break many women came to me to share how Jesus had ministered to them as they opened their hearts to encounter more of His Presence. It was a common statement from them that they prayed, but never listened to learn what was on God's heart.

The afternoon session on 'Restoring the Soul', which included part of my own journey following the rape, brought understanding to many. They had never heard of God getting down into the roots of their hurts and brokenness to bring restoration to their lives. Again, the altar was packed with those who desired ministry. Deep restorations took place over the next hour and a half.

Many ladies asked for appointments for personal ministry. I was amazed that they were willing to drive two hours to the city, spend two hours having ministry and then drive home again. It demonstrated the great need for the ministry of restoration.

At the close of the Conference I was approached to share at a Women's Conference in Clare - another country town. This time, God led me to share on 'Experiencing the Love of the Father' and 'Dwelling in the Secret Place'. I was conscious of God's determination to take us deeper into Him than ever before. What a privilege His children have, to be called to experience His love and Presence in greater ways than previous generations.

In the morning session on *"Experiencing the Love of the Father,"* I taught on the privilege it is to be called the children of God. Father God has lavished His love upon us but I believe many of us need a revelation of that. It's not just that 'God so loves the world', but that God loves me and you, individually. Only as the disciples watched Jesus living out His life before them as God's Son did they begin to understand what it meant to have a personal relationship with God as Father. Only Jesus Christ as Son can reveal God to us as our Father. We are dependent upon the grace that comes to us through Jesus. The Fatherhood of God is the source of our personal identity. Multitudes would run into His arms if the Church today could effectively communicate the reality of God as a loving Father,.

Only recently have I begun to think of Heaven as my home. What I remember most about the time I was taken up into Heaven was the experience of God's overwhelming love. I could feel it all over me. During another time of renewal, over a 40 day period, I experienced many outpourings of His love. Because of experiencing God's love, I now know that I will simply 'change my address' when I leave this earth. This is not because I am special, or have laboured long in the Kingdom of God, but simply because I have received His love.

Picture a little child held securely in his father's arms. Even with much happening around him, the child is totally at peace, unconcerned about everything else – secure in his father's arms. When we are secure in the love of the Father we run to Him when problems arise. There is absolutely nothing we can do to cause God to love us any more or any less – His love is unconditional except for the necessity of being willing to receive it! God is love and we were created for love – to experience it with our heavenly Father and with human beings. The response to the altar call showed that it was the first time many had heard that they could experience Father's Love. For others, it was an opportunity for a fresh encounter with that love. How wonderful it was to experience God's love poured out so generously!

After the lunchbreak I spoke about *"Dwelling in the Secret Place."*

For many years I had been drawn by Holy Spirit to passages of Scripture concerning the 'secret place' **(Psalm 91:1, Psalm 27:5,**

Song of Songs 2:10-14). I believe it is where God wants every believer to be. When we understand what this means, we are well on our way to living under an open Heaven, which means Heaven will impact our lives right here and now.

Father God invites us to **dwell** in the secret place, not just wander in occasionally. Can you imagine what it would be like to live in that place – right in His Presence? God desires us to be there in that 'secret place' with Him. In **Psalm 31:20** the Lord is saying He will hide us in that secret place away from all evil!

He desires to share intimacy and love with us in that secret place. He desires to hear our voice and to see our face. I don't know about you but my heart responds to His desire, and I, too, want to be there, hearing His wonderful voice and seeing the One who is altogether lovely. I have found that as I seek His Presence more diligently I am not always asking Him to do something for me, but rather yielding to Him and asking "Lord, here I am, but what's on **Your** heart?" God draws us toward that secret place – the secret place of the Most High. He draws us, but we must choose to come.

In **Jeremiah 29:13** it says *'I will seek Your face, Lord.'* It does not say I will seek Your hand. When we seek His face we are interested in Who He is; when we seek His hand we are preoccupied with what He can do for us! This was an incredible revelation to me. Such an awareness of His Presence has been birthed in me. It is so wonderful.

I'm sure you have all heard that expression *'you become like those you live with'*. It is my greatest desire that I change the atmosphere wherever I go simply because I carry God's Presence. We carry His Presence as a result of dwelling with Him in that secret place. It is God's will for us – it's our inheritance. The price for it has been paid. Jesus purchased it for us on the Cross. Let us allow time in our daily lives to meet Him in that secret place.

Once again, the altar was packed and the Lord poured out His Presence in such a way that I couldn't stand without support. Humbling ourselves before God, and repenting of our self-centeredness, enabled Holy Spirit to lead us into the secret place of His Presence where our focus was on Him, the King or Kings and the Lord of Lords!

Following this conference I was approached to present my Prayer Ministry Training at Influencers Church in Clare over a five month period. It proved to be a fruitful time for all involved and left its mark on that church's prayer team. During that time I was privileged, too, to engage in mentoring the prayer team's leader.

The following year I was asked to speak at the Women's Conference in Clare again, and this time the Lord gave me **"Becoming a Friend of God"** as the theme. In the morning session He instructed me to speak on **"Knowing God as our Father"**. It is one thing to know from the Word of God that God is our Father, which makes us His children, but it is quite another to live in the reality of it. Oh, what a privilege! **1 John 3:1-2 'Behold, what manner of love the Father has bestowed upon us, that we should be called the children of God: Beloved, now we are children of God . . . we shall become like Him'.** We need revelation that He is not an impersonal God, somewhere far off in a distant Heaven, but He's our loving Father, who embraces us as His precious children.

We cannot see God the same as we view our earthly father. Some of us had good fathers, others didn't. I used to see God sitting on His throne with a ruler in His hand just waiting for me to make a mistake – then, smack, smack! My challenge at the end of the session was: "How would you measure your relationship with Father God? Is it one of love, security and intimacy, or one of insecurity and distance, even fear? Are you longing for a closer, more intimate relationship with God as your Father?

I believe God's heart for us today is *'I want to be your friend – do you want to be My friend?'* We can ask God to remove any barriers that would prevent us having a personal relationship with Him." The tangible love of God manifested in the room that day, and many lives were transformed. What a wonderful, loving Father He is!

During the lunch break a lady handed me an envelope containing $250. She explained that I had ministered to her and her husband 25 years ago when their marriage was failing. God had healed and restored them and they wanted to bless me for the marriage they were still enjoying. Such testimonies are a wonderful blessing when you are in ministry.

The second session addressed **"Friendship with God"**. This Friendship is the one we need more than any other. He did everything for us in giving us His Son. On the Cross, Jesus made the Great Exchange:

> *He was punished – that we might be forgiven*
> *He was wounded – that we might be healed*
> *He was made sin with our sinfulness – that we might be made righteous*
> *He died our death – that we might receive His life*
> *He was made a curse – that we might enter into the blessing*
> *He endured our poverty – that we might have abundance*
> *He bore our shame – that we might share His glory*
> *He endured our rejection – for our acceptance from the Father*
> *Our old nature was put to death – so that we have a new nature*

Do you know any other friend who would do that for you? Father God is the best Friend. He is always there for us. We belong to Him because He paid a great price for us. We need to know Him intimately, but the only way to get to know any friend is to spend time with them. So what is intimacy? It's a close and warm friendship, a personal, private, loving, affectionate relationship where we share our innermost thoughts and feelings. Is that how you would describe your relationship with God?

Knowing *about* God is not truly *knowing* Him. God created us for intimacy – a walking, talking relationship. Religion *con*forms us – to a set of rules, but relationship *trans*forms us – into the image of Jesus! So how do we build this type of relationship of respect, trust and communication? **Psalm 46:10** gives us the answer **– "Be still and know that I am God"**. In our busy world that seems to be easier said than done doesn't it? However, if we value God as our Friend, we will make time to be with Him just as we do for our earthly friends. One of the benefits of intimacy with God is that we fall in love with Him like never before, we walk with Him and talk with Him and we become like Him! Let us not miss out on the rich pleasure of knowing Him as our best friend.

The enemy works hard to rob us of time spent with God. He knows if he gets that, he gets everything! As we learn to cultivate friendship with God we will become more sensitive to Holy Spirit and experience breakthroughs that unveil heavenly realities to us. It brings us into divine favour with God and access to all that He is – and has! He calls us to spend time alone with Him so He can plant seeds of revival and power within us.

My closing challenge was, "Will you make Father God *your* best friend today and choose to have intimate friendship with Him from this day onwards?" And many did become true friends of God that afternoon. As I prayed with one person after another, the power of God manifested to such a degree that we must have looked drunk! What a privilege it is to be a vessel of the Lord God to minister His love, Presence and power to others. As a result of the Conference there were many changed lives and relationships with God taken to new levels. How wonderful to discover that our God is One who wants us as friends, not as mere servants.

Not long after I had completed the Seminar in Clare I was invited to present my Prayer Ministry Course (the four levels plus the one day of Practical Training) at Impact Church, Tanunda in the Barossa Valley. It was received well and the feedback was awesome. Ps Trevor and Valmai Auricht were incredible hosts and many lives were touched and transformed during the Seminar. I will never forget reading through the Confidential Course Evaluations when I arrived home. They were so encouraging, at times I wondered if it was really me they were talking about! I celebrated the goodness of God. He can do anything through anybody if we will simply follow His directions. All glory to our wonderful Father God!

Invitations to minister continue. 'Word of mouth' is powerful, and one of the reasons I choose not to have a website or any other form of advertisement. To this day, I continue teaching at seminars and conferences, preaching, and in 'one-on-one' prayer ministry. When the Lord opens doors for you, no man can close them.

Chapter 15
CONCLUSION

I often have a bit of a laugh over the fact that as a young person I took a course in Public Speaking, thinking I might be good at it. That bright idea went right out the window when I failed the practical component, but of course, I had absolutely no idea, then, what God had in store for me. However, God's Word says *"Whatever the enemy means for evil, God will turn it around for good" (Genesis 50:20).* As I bring the story of my life's journey to a close, I can't help but be amazed at what our loving Heavenly Father has done with a life that was so broken as to be almost beyond repair.

And when I look at the way God is still using me today, it's hard to believe where I came from. I can say in all honesty that I do not regret that my life was shattered for over twenty years following the rape. Because of it, I learned the keys of how God heals and restores broken souls. Because of it I know that we can't deal with the visible symptoms of brokenness by ignoring it or burying it. Bad roots bear bad fruit, which affects our soul. We need Him to reveal the roots of the bad fruit (e.g. anger, fear, bitterness) in our lives. Only God can do that. My life is such a testimony of the reality of that Old Testament verse in **Genesis 50**.

The healing of our souls is such a vital area in our growth as a child of God. If there are areas in our souls left unhealed, they will hinder our intimacy with God (e.g. rejection will isolate us from close relationships). Unhealed, we will struggle to relate to find friendship with God because we don't feel good enough, and we will never walk in the fullness of God's love for us. We can freely enter into these and many other areas of our walk with God as we are healed from such hindrances.

It is my prayer that dealing with these root causes will become imperative in the Christian life, so that all will walk in the fullness of what the Spirit of God intends for us. Of course, it is vital to deal with the salvation of the unsaved, but, equally, room should be made for healing wounded souls as part of that full salvation. I am 75 at the time of writing. Many people ask why I am still teaching, preaching and doing personal Prayer Ministry consultations at my age. Apart from the fact that it is the call of God on my life, it is also the cry of my heart. When one has been as hurt and broken as I was, and then graciously restored by a loving Heavenly Father, how could I not be passionate about seeing others fully healed and restored?

My passion for what I do is certainly put to that test when I am presenting Prayer Ministry Training. For each of the four levels of the Training I am on my feet Friday evening from 7.00 – 9.30 pm and Saturday from 9.00 am until 4.30 pm with only a half hour sit down for lunch. The Practical Level is conducted over a whole Saturday, too. Yet, I am never tired, my feet don't ache and my mouth has never stopped functioning yet! That's what passion can do for you.

It is not by accident this book has come into your hands. May I close by asking you, the reader, a question? Did anything I have written expose some hidden wounding in your soul? If so, please seek out help from somebody who deals with healing and restoration of the soul. Trust me, the journey is worth it all. Your relationship with Jesus and Father God will go to a brand new level – one so intimate, loving and exciting, you will wonder how you ever lived without it!

If you have not yet invited Jesus Christ into your life as your Lord and Saviour and you want to receive all that He has done for you, you may do so by praying the following prayer out loud:

Lord Jesus,

Thank You for loving me and dying for me on the Cross.

Your precious Blood washes me clean from every sin.

You are my Lord and my Saviour, now and forever.

I believe You rose from the dead and that You are alive today.

Because of Your finished work,

I am now a beloved child of God and heaven is my home.

Thank You for giving me eternal life

and filling my heart with Your peace and joy.

Amen

NEED SUPPORT?

If the themes discussed in this book have raised concerns for you or someone you know, please contact:

Lifeline 13 11 14 www.lifeline.org.au
Beyond Blue 1300 22 4636 www.beyondblue.org.au
Blue Knot Foundation 1300 657 380 www.blueknot.org.au

Professional counselling services can be found at
Christian Counsellors Association of Australia www.ccaa.net.au

Chapter 16
TESTIMONIES

Alan and I have been extremely blessed to be used as servants of a God who cares so much for the bruised and broken and for those in bondage. That's why Jesus came - to make a way for us to be restored and made whole. It has been our privilege to witness the hand of God at work in thousands of lives. It has been an exciting journey for us and we have learned so much as we have walked this way with the Lord. We know without a shadow of a doubt that these testimonies are not because of who we are, but rather because of who God is, and we give Him all the glory.

Satanic Ritual Abuse Child Totally Healed and Restored!

I feel to finish the story I touched on earlier, about the child who was ritually abused by satanists; the situation which revealed my own need in that area. I continued to minister to this young girl, even while re-living my own memories. Elfie (one of my valued team members) and I were amazed at the way God moved through me even though I was going through my own difficult journey. Over many months we continued to minister to her as God directed and, eventually, she was healed and totally restored emotionally and mentally. Praise the Lord Jesus Christ who paid the price with His Blood so that we can be healed, restored and set free!

Testimony of deliverance

A number of years ago we received a phone call from a gentleman seeking ministry for his sister. She had been in a mental institution for eight years and had spent much time in solitude because of her aggressive behaviour. She even burned the medical staff with her cigarettes. Alan and I were reluctant to minister in this area because we felt totally inadequate. However, the gentleman believed God had directed him to us and so we finally agreed. We called another husband and wife on our team to join us. We didn't have great faith (rather fear and trepidation!) but we did have confidence in the goodness of God.

The lady arrived with her husband and we listened to the journey she had taken since the birth of her only child. She had an uncontrollable urge to kill her baby. This was so strong that only when she took up a knife and killed one of the white rabbits, which they bred, would the desire to kill leave her for a season. This happened on a number of occasions and after receiving psychiatric help over a period of time with no real breakthrough, she was institutionalised. All the time she was speaking, we noticed there was a switch of facial expressions and voice changes. We were aware we were dealing with the demonic. Help, God was our silent prayer.

Bit by bit, precious Holy Spirit unravelled the mystery. He showed us that this lady had been a twin in her mother's womb. Her mother underwent abortion, but because they were unaware there were twins, only one baby was aborted. In a vision the Lord showed us a black shape attached to the remaining baby - our client - in the womb. When we enquired what that was, God identified it as a spirit of murder. We commanded that spirit to lose its hold and after a short battle the lady was totally and completely free. Praise You Jesus!

When this lady came back for her follow-up appointment her countenance was so changed we hardly recognised her. She shared with us the best illustration I have ever heard on the 'Grace of God'. This demonstrated to us that Prayer Ministry is definitely not about how much knowledge we have, but all about allowing the Holy Spirit to give revelation and then Him doing things His way.

Several months later this lady had the opportunity to speak to her mother about what the Lord had revealed and her mother confirmed it. There was forgiveness and restoration of a relationship that had always been rather distant. It is the heart of our loving Heavenly Father to bind up every broken heart and set every captive free. We are simply His vessels.

Man Released from a Mental Institution

Recently, a local Pastor asked me to come alongside a lady who was going through a very difficult time. Her son was in a mental institution and she was not coping with that. I was simply to spend time encouraging her, but the call of God in me wanted to go deeper and get down to the roots in her son's life. It was not possible to minister to him personally so I sought God for His strategy.

God showed me the roots of insanity, sexual sin and child sacrifice in the son's generational line, as well as a few other issues. Next time his mother came I shared with her that God had revealed some roots that needed attending to. She was a nominal Christian and I knew she would not understand what I was talking about, but I told her that God could break the power of these things as I prayed and took authority in Jesus' name. I asked her if she would come into agreement as I prayed even though she did not understand, because the Word of God tells us that if two agree together on anything, it will be done. She agreed and so I prayed as God led me to and she simply said 'yes and amen' to each area I took authority over to break its power.

About five weeks later she contacted me with the miracle news that her son had just been discharged from the mental institution. The authorities there could not explain what had happened to him, but for just over a month his behaviour had been perfectly normal. Praise the wonderful name of Jesus Christ!

Testimony of a Restored Marriage (1)

Alan and I were ministering to a lady who was having difficulties in her marriage. The Lord Jesus had healed many of her own rejections and abuses from her childhood and relationships, but her husband refused to attend because he felt there was no hope for restoration. They were a Christian couple but were unable to reconcile their differences.

One evening she came to the door with her husband. We invited them in, but he said he was not staying. In fact, he was leaving her that very night. He already had his car and trailer loaded with his possessions. We knew the situation was serious, but we also knew our God was more than able to step in at the eleventh hour and turn things around. I was prompted by the Spirit to ask him to come in for just a moment and after some hesitation he decided that he would. His wife was extremely upset so I took her aside, calmed her down and we agreed that we would trust God together. She had nothing to lose and everything to gain.

We served coffee and began to chat. As we talked the Lord gave us revelation of the problems which he had brought into the marriage. We carefully asked questions until the admission of these things came from his own mouth. He repented to the Lord for all the things he thought did not affect anybody but himself. He also asked his wife to forgive him for his part in the marriage breakdown. It was the first time he had ever taken any responsibility. That was the first breakthrough which enabled him to choose not to leave her.

Over the following weeks of Prayer Ministry with them as a couple we saw the Lord Jesus take both of them back to the traumas and pain in their past, healing and delivering them from the bondages of the enemy. It was a privilege to watch Jesus gently take these two broken lives, gather up all the pieces and mould them into a beautiful, joyful couple so much in love with each other and with Jesus.

This couple attended our Prayer Ministry Training and became part of our Prayer Ministry Team. They served with us together for a number of years and we were thrilled to watch the way the Lord used them, especially in the area of bringing healing and restoration to broken marriages.

Testimony of a Restored Marriage (2)

A very sad gentleman arrived for ministry. His marriage had broken down and he and his wife had separated, pending divorce. We ministered to his hurts which gave him a measure of healing and restoration for his soul. At the prompting of Holy Spirit, I suggested to him that he ask his wife to come with him on his next visit. 'Why don't you tell her I'd love to meet her?' I said. He said he would ask her, but insisted she would not come. Before the next session, Alan and I prayed that she would attend.

Sure enough, they came together for the next appointment. At the beginning it was as though we were trying to break through a brick wall. The wife sat with arms folded, her body language saying 'there's nothing you can say or do to break through here – I've made up my mind it's over'. I thank God for a sense of humour that eventually broke down the barriers until many issues between them came to the surface. After a number of visits, they were re-united and have remained happily together for more than ten years. Thank You Jesus that You are the God of breakthrough!

Ministry to the Mentally Retarded

I was asked to pray with a young girl who was mentally retarded. I met with her and her mother (a clergyman's wife) at my friend's home for morning tea, followed by prayer. Early that morning I prayed for revelation, but all I received from the Lord was a scripture about salvation. I was disappointed because I expected more. After all, this girl could not communicate!

I was sipping my coffee, praying in my head, only half listening to the girl's mother. I nearly choked when she started talking about some meetings where there were several salvations. There was that word again! I was prompted to ask if her daughter had given her heart to Jesus. She stared back in disbelief that I would even ask. 'No', she said. I asked if I could speak to the little girl about Jesus.

The mother was apprehensive but she nodded agreement, so I sat down on the floor where the child was playing and asked her slowly and clearly if she knew who Jesus was. She nodded her head, so I continued by telling her that Jesus loved her so very much and wanted to come and live in her heart. When I asked if she would like that she nodded again. Her mother was clearly amazed. I continued *'I will pray a prayer on your behalf asking Jesus to come into your heart, and if you agree with what I am saying just nod your head. If you don't agree, shake your head.'* She nodded as if she understood, so I prayed a 'sinners prayer'. She nodded vigorously all the way through.

When I said *'Amen'* her face suddenly lit up with a beautiful smile. I sheepishly got up off the floor and sat at the table with my friend and the girl's mother. Her mother looked at me in amazement. Suddenly, the child started pounding her chest quite hard and repeating the name of Jesus. Now the mother was really paying attention. Her daughter had never said that before. I was still getting my head around the fact that God had just saved a severely mentally retarded child, so I asked her, *'Where is Jesus?'* She pounded herself on the chest and again her face lit up with that beautiful smile. That was it! Her mother, my friend and I finally realised that God had gifted this little mentally retarded child with salvation.

The last report we had from her mother was that even though she is still retarded, she has progressed in many areas. Previously, she had no sense of balance, but now she rides a bicycle and enjoys ballet lessons. Because of the severity of her retardation, she had been assessed as unsuitable for speech therapy, but is now learning to communicate with words.

What a lesson I had that day about the sovereignty of God. Salvation is not a decision we make with our mind, but in our hearts in response to the Spirit of God.

Two Year Old Delivered from Murder and Abortion

I was asked to minister to a two year old girl who seemed to have two different sides to her personality. I was a little reluctant due to her age, but her mother seemed desperate for answers, so I finally agreed. One side of this child was most beautiful. People in cafes and shopping centres would stop and comment on how adorable she was. The other side was quite the opposite. For no apparent reason she would suddenly switch to shouting, screaming, and throwing herself around in uncontrollable behaviours. It was like chalk and cheese!

I placed a mat on the floor with some colouring in books and pencils so she could focus on that instead of just sitting there while I ministered. When I began to pray and ask God for the root causes of her behaviour the first insight was that a spirit of murder and a spirit of abortion were involved. This was surprising. When I shared this with the mother she seemed confused, but she agreed for me to continue with what God had shown me.

I dealt with some other generational strongholds first and that went well, but when I began to command the spirit of murder to leave, the response was an incredible demonic manifestation in the child. I could scarcely believe what I saw. I had never seen such evil in the eyes of any adult I had ministered to, let alone a child. Making no progress with the spirit of murder I changed my command to the spirit of abortion, but still there was no release. Now I was confused because this had never ever happened in all my years of ministry.

I took a few moments break and began again. In the midst of taking authority over the works of satan I 'accidently' commanded the spirit of murder and abortion to leave in the same sentence. This time, it was as though satan himself stared at me through her eyes. I knew God had given 'on the job' revelation, so I kept commanding both murder and abortion to leave together. With one last violent manifestation they left the child. She got up from the floor, came over to me, climbed onto my lap and put her arms around my neck. Her mother and I could hardly believe the change in her countenance. I was having difficulty understanding what had happened so I asked the mother what had preceded the child's birth. She explained she had had four pregnancies. The first, a son, was healthy, but the second child died within days of birth from severe congenital problems. Pregnant with a third child, tests revealed that it had the same disease as the second one, and she chose to abort it, hence the entry of a spirit of abortion. She also disclosed that a family member had been jailed for the crime of murder. Both of these spirits had been passed down to the fourth child, the little girl.

This beautiful child has never looked back. She is a lovable child with a delightful personality. I praise God for what I learnt through ministering to her.

Two Malaysian Ladies Delivered From Occult Bondage
We received a phone call from two young women asking if they could make appointments for ministry with us when they came to Australia for their holidays. Even though Christianity was illegal in their country at that time, we sensed they were serious about their walk with Jesus. We agreed to see them and set aside a whole week to accommodate them.

We were amazed how far these delightful Asian girls had already come in their walk with the Lord Jesus. They were committed to being clean, whole and free before Him. We had rarely seen such a passion for God, for His holiness and His Kingdom. It was a privilege to minister to them. And God was faithful to show us how to minister. He gave us many visions of cultural ceremonies which they had participated in before becoming Christians, and showed us how these ceremonies had entangled them in demonic bondage. The process of setting them free from all cultural and demonic bondages was so simple because of their passion and hunger for the Lord Jesus Christ. Revelations from Holy Spirit came one after the other as they repented before the Lord for their pre-Christian sin and ungodly cultural practices. The Lord showed us fetishes hidden in their homes as protection against evil spirits, their participation in the dance of the dragon - a cultural celebration – and many other incidences where bondages were rooted. They thought we did a marvellous job of ministering, but we knew it was God, through His Holy Spirit, who did the work of healing their broken hearts, setting them free from the bondages of satan and bringing total healing and restoration to their lives.

Before they flew back home they requested a set of DVDs of our Prayer Ministry Training to take back to Malaysia. They knew it would be difficult to get Christian material through customs, but we all prayed that Lord Jesus who makes eyes to see, could also make seeing eyes blind as they went through customs! And that was exactly what happened. They shared the teaching with the underground Church, and as a result, many people were healed both physically and emotionally, and many were set free from the bondage of the enemy.

PERSONAL TESTIMONIES
(all names changed to protect privacy)

Ian - South Australia
A friend suggested he bring Alan and Lee to my home to pray with me. I did not believe in God at all, let alone that He could heal me of cancer. Not wanting to offend my friend and also thinking there just might be a 'chance', I reluctantly agreed.

When Alan and Lee came to pray the day before my surgery, I remember thinking 'they don't look all that weird'. I listened as Lee shared about the love of God and what Jesus had accomplished for me on the Cross and for the first time in my life I believed and received Jesus as my Saviour. Lee was about to pray for my stomach cancer when she hesitated and asked me if there were any unresolved issues in my life such as unforgiveness, broken relationships, any unresolved hurts or pain, or even grief that had not been resolved. I couldn't even answer. I just sobbed and sobbed until I was spent. (I learned afterwards that the unresolved grief was released that day!) She gently led me in a prayer letting go of the unforgiveness I had held against the person who had hurt me, and then prayed for my healing.

I awoke from the surgery to remove my stomach cancer to be greeted by a puzzled doctor who told me they had found no cancer when they opened me up. I met Jesus as my Healer that day. Praise Him!

Jan – South Australia

Lee was speaking at a Christian Camp which I attended. I was very 'down' as my younger brother's wife was about to give birth to their first baby. My husband and I had tried to conceive for over eight years without success. During the camp Lee had a vision of my husband and me standing under the shade of a tree holding a baby. Because of the sensitivity of the situation she shared it first with my mother who encouraged her to tell me. I was almost too afraid to believe, but I sensed an excitement within my spirit. Within a few months I was pregnant.

When our baby was about six months old my husband and I visited Alan and Lee. We were proudly showing them our photo album with the photos of the baby in from birth onwards, when Lee exclaimed, 'There it is' and pointed to a photo of my husband and I under a tree and holding the baby. It was exactly the same as the vision Lee had seen nearly a year earlier. We praise God for the faithfulness of God in not only giving us the desires of our hearts but also encouraging our faith with a prophetic vision.

Jayne – South Australia
It is now been nearly two months since I came for Prayer Ministry. When I first returned home I had to visit my GP who has known me for nine years. Even though he was busy he couldn't stop asking me why I looked so well. I was able to share with him the healing and ministry I had received at Fresh Wine International. I shared how I was healed and set free from the roots of my emotional problems by revelation of the Holy Spirit, and also how much Jesus meant to me and what a difference He had made in my life.

Andrew – South Australia
I had battled with lust for as long as I can remember. A friend suggested I contact Alan and Lee for ministry. I had received much ministry during the seven years I had been a Christian, yet nothing had changed, so I was both reluctant and sceptical. During Prayer Ministry the Holy Spirit revealed that there was a curse of illegitimacy over our family line and that I had inherited a spirit of lust. Alan and Lee broke the curse off me and my family line. I was delivered from the spirit of lust that night and have been totally free ever since. Praise the Lord!

Janet – South Australia
I had an abortion when I was younger and had lived with the guilt and shame of that ever since. When I was ministered to at Fresh Wine International, I was treated with respect, love and mercy, rather than the judgment I had previously received. I received God's forgiveness, forgave myself and was totally healed.

Sharon – South Australia
You would think that having a baby would be the most wonderful experience you could imagine. Mine was a nightmare. My baby boy was always happy and peaceful when out amongst the family

activities, but the moment we placed him in his cot in his room, regardless of whether it was day or night, he would scream relentlessly until we removed him from his room. Sleepless nights and desperation led us to call Alan and Lee to our home. After Holy Spirit revealed to Lee that the swinging mobile above his cot had a demonic influence attached, we destroyed it and have never had a single re-occurrence of the screaming. We now enjoy peace in our home. Thank you.

Jenny – South Australia

My life was shattered through sin and pain and in deep depression when I came to Fresh Wine for ministry. Thank God He still binds up broken hearts and sets captives free from emotional pain caused from deep hurts which wounded my soul. Jesus took the pieces of my broken heart and wounded soul, healing and restoring them and putting them back together, making me whole again.

Beverly – South Australia

My husband 'forced' me to go to Alan and Lee for ministry. Our marriage of three years was on the rocks because I could not enter into intimate relationship and two years of counselling had failed to produce any results. During Prayer Ministry revelation of incest in my childhood was revealed by Holy Spirit. My soul was healed and restored and I was set free. I now enjoy a great marriage with my wonderful husband and our three beautiful children. Praise God!

Heather – South Australia

I came to Fresh Wine for healing for a cancerous growth in my left breast. Holy Spirit revealed that the root cause was a curse coming down my generational line. As the power of the curse was broken and I received prayer for healing, the lump disappeared immediately. Thank God for His wonderful grace and divine healing.

David - South Australia

My mother who was not a Christian took me to see Alan and Lee. I was so overwhelmed by grief after the loss of my young wife that I was unable to function. After receiving a revelation of the Father's love and receiving His healing for my wounded soul during Prayer Ministry, I was totally restored. When my mother witnessed the reality of a living God, she gave her heart to the Lord. I have since remarried and have two beautiful children.

Pastor W - South Australia

Thank God for those in the Body of Christ who have the heart to allow God to uncover the roots of ungodly behaviours, such as my outrageous anger, exposing them to the light and bringing the Cross of Jesus to bear upon them. My life was transformed when Alan and Lee prayed for me for healing of the memories. Thank you so much.

Jenny - South Australia

I was a diabetic and had been addicted to drugs for some time. I had a desire to be free from it all but nobody seemed able to help. That is until somebody told me about Fresh Wine International. So I made an appointment and went along hoping for a change in my life. I was blown away when the team told me what God had shown them was the root causes of my condition. God had revealed that there was alcoholic addiction in the bloodline, which leads to sugar addiction and then progressing to other sorts of addictions such as drugs.

They began ministry by breaking the general curse of addiction, and then cleansing the bloodline with the Blood of Jesus. They took authority over the addiction that led to diabetes and then broke the drug addiction. After that they prayed for my soul to be completely healed and restored from all the damage caused through my addiction and diabetes. To this day I have no sign of diabetes at all and have never taken drugs of any description since. Praise the Lord for those who hear what God says and apply it to people to bring healing, freedom and total restoration. Thank You Heavenly Father.

Pastor G – Victoria

I flew over to see you both because I was too ashamed of my addiction to admit to anybody, let alone seek ministry, in my own state. Thank you so much for providing a 'safe place' for people like me to come and allowing the Spirit of God to flow through you bringing healing and deliverance. God bless you both and your ministry too.

Cheryl – Victoria

You prayed over me for healing for my sister who had been unable to conceive a child for the last two and a half years. She's pregnant! While you were praying for me I felt a strong assurance that there would be a baby before Christmas. The next day I rang my mother and explained briefly what happened and passed on that assurance. And now on the first cycle after we prayed, my sister is pregnant. She knows what happened and she and her husband are really praising God too.

Kristina – Victoria

I thank God for the ministry team at Fresh Wine International. After several appointments I was healed from abandonment, as I was an adopted child. My life has been totally healed, my marriage restored and I am now ministering in the area of healing and restoration in my own Church.

Robert – Victoria

Our marriage was a mess and I was ready to run when my wife pleaded with me to attend just one appointment at Fresh Wine International. I went just to get her off my back thinking I could leave once I'd been. During Prayer Ministry the Lord revealed the rejection I had received as a child by a teacher at school, which was the root of my anger which had almost destroyed my life and our marriage. Thank God He is the God of the second chance!

Pastor K – New South Wales

I was so ashamed of my addiction to pornography that I flew in from Sydney to see Alan and Lee so nobody would know about it. I heard from friends that they could be trusted to keep everything inside the four walls. I was wonderfully released as they dealt with the root cause of sexual abuse as a child and I have been serving God in purity ever since.

Emma – New South Wales

I had battled with sickness and disease as long as I could remember. It was just one thing after another and sometimes the medical profession could find absolutely no cause for my symptoms. It was suggested that I might need some psychiatric help. I found this suggestion offensive because I knew the pain and other symptoms were very real. At Fresh Wine International I was set free from a generational curse of infirmity and the demon of affliction which had been assigned to me and my family line. Since receiving ministry, I have not had a sick day, not even the flu. Praise the Lord for my complete healing and His wonderful gift of Divine health.

Barry – New South Wales

During a short plane trip interstate, I sat next to a total stranger – Lee Habbershaw. By the time I reached my destination I had invited Jesus Christ into my life and was so excited about the many things Lee shared with me about her relationship with God, and all the things He had done in her own life and through her ministry. I thank God for allowing a 'Divine appointment' with Lee to help me begin the journey I have been on with the Lord ever since.

David – Queensland

When I was in Adelaide holidaying with my sister I happened to mention the terrible nightmares and unusual sensations of 'somebody present' which had been happening since the death of our mother several years earlier. She suggested I make an appointment with Fresh Wine as she had previously had some Prayer Ministry with them with excellent results.

During the ministry time, after the Prayer Ministers had dealt with the area of grief, Lee had a vision of a jewellery box which she described in detail. I was dumbfounded as it was an exact description of one my mother had given me just prior to her death. Lee explained how we can be tied to the person who had owned the object, and even though I was not sure about that we broke the ties. When I returned home to Brisbane the nightmares stopped and 'presence' in the house was gone. I praise God for His servants who function in the gifts of the Holy Spirit.

Pastor W – Western Australia

I attended Prayer Ministry Training in 1998 at Christian Counselling College which was founded by Alan and Lee Habbershaw. During the Training my life was pulled to pieces, rearranged and put back together by the power of the Holy Spirit. I had always been a person who functioned by formulas and I appreciated the sensitivity to the Spirit of God by Lee and the team. It was by revelation of the Holy Spirit that the roots of major problems in my life (including that of an orphan spirit caused through not being a wanted child) were brought to the surface and dealt with once and for all.

Today I am married to a Pastor, have been blessed with four children and we have an active Prayer Ministry Team in our Church. Thank you so much for being 'pioneers' in this area of ministry, Alan and Lee. God bless you both.

Jason – Tasmania

Some years ago I attended Christian Counselling College to complete the Prayer Ministry Training and loved every minute of it. Lee and the other teachers were continually emphasising that there are no formulas in ministry, but it is Holy Spirit Who gives revelation. This truth alone changed my thinking forever. I have since moved to Tasmania where I am the leader of the Prayer Ministry Team in our Church. I am so fulfilled in what I am doing. Thank you so much.

Chris – Queensland

I came to Adelaide for ministry with Fresh Wine as my father is a well-known Christian leader in my state. Although he appeared to be the 'perfect Christian' to others, he was a totally different person at home. As long as I can remember he abused me in just every possible way. The verbal abuse as a child crushed my spirit even more than the physical abuse. The spiritual abuse of being told God made a big mistake when He made me, and that He could never love me because I simply didn't measure up, caused me to have a totally unhealthy view of God.

During the ministry the team broke the curse of words spoken against me and God healed my broken and bruised soul from the trauma of abuse. I was able to forgive my father when God revealed through the team that he was a broken man himself.

After I was fully healed and restored my father started to notice the change in my life and I could see he was trying to treat me like a son but still having difficulty. Eventually he asked me what had happened to bring such a radical change in my life. When I shared with him what had taken place during the ministry with Fresh Wine International, he chose to make an appointment and was eventually healed and restored himself. Thank you, Fresh Wine, for obeying the call of God on your lives. God bless you.

Mr Supajo – Solo, Indonesia

I had lived in fear and shame for many years because of shock and trauma and the emotional and physical hurts I received as a child, but through listening to the testimony of Mrs Lee, which she included in her Prayer Training Seminar, I was able to give my burden to Jesus and my heart is filled with joy and peace.

Emily (Women's Refuge) – Jakarta, Indonesia

My life was a mess. I had many problems and my life was so miserable. Then I attended a Seminar held by Fresh Wine in Jakarta. During this time I heard how God was my friend and wanted to help me. Through the preaching of God's Word satan's power was broken and my life turned around. After my baby is born I want to tell my family of the change in me and that I want to live for Jesus. Thank you, Fresh Wine.

Ratna – Bogor, Indonesia

I have lived the Christian life from a child but suffered rejection from my family. It is not easy to be a woman in my country. But through the ministry of Fresh Wine International God began a work in me. Every day of their Seminar I received healing and courage as God's Holy Spirit worked through the Fresh Wine team. Thank you for spending time with me and encouraging me to be all God wants me to be.

Theresia – Bogor, Indonesia

I was a prostitute and had lived a promiscuous life. After I had given my life to Jesus I still suffered from depression and a sense that satan still had power over my life. A witchdoctor had inserted needles into my body and face, not visible to the eye, in order to get customers for my profession (it attracted them like a magnet). Through the ministry of Fresh Wine, I was completely set free from the power of satan. The needles the witchdoctor had inserted fell out two weeks after the prayer and I have been living for Jesus ever since.